Today and Tomorrow in America

Books by Martin Mayer

NONFICTION

Today and Tomorrow in America
Conflicts of Interest: Broker-Dealer Firms
The Bankers
About Television
Bricks, Mortar and the Performing Arts
New Breed on Wall Street
(with Cornell Capa)
All You Know Is Facts
The Teachers Strike: New York 1968
Diploma: International Schools and University Entrance
Emory Buckner
The Lawyers
Social Studies in American Schools
The Schools
Madison Avenue, U.S.A.
Wall Street: Men and Money

FICTION

A Voice That Fills the House
The Experts

Today and Tomorrow in America

MARTIN MAYER

HARPER & ROW, PUBLISHERS
New York, Evanston, San Francisco, London

To our boys, now men—
but not quite yet their own men—
for whom this book
may be a bit of a nuisance

A portion of this work appeared originally in somewhat different form in *Commentary.*

Designed by C. Linda Dingler

Library of Congress Cataloging in Publication Data

Mayer, Martin, 1928–
  Today and tomorrow in America.

    1. United States—Social conditions. 2. United States—Economic conditions. 3. United States—Civilization. I. Title.
HN55.M39   309.1'73   73–14273
ISBN 0–06–012872–0

First Edition

76 77 78 79 10 9 8 7 6 5 4 3 2 1

Contents

The middle-class pessimism over the future of the world comes from a confusion between civilization and security.

—Alfred N. Whitehead

1

Surprise!

*I am absolutely convinced that the developed economies
have turned a great corner. Owing to the fabulous
proliferation of our technology, owing to the incredible
possibilities of unlimited energy, owing to the computer
and the automative revolution which are just beginning,
we are not short of resources. On the contrary, it's going
to be devising means to use these resources, to put these
resources to work, which is going to be the great
challenge of the next twenty years.*

—Barbara Ward, 1964

*The intimate, inescapable interdependence of living
things implies a certain stability, a certain dynamic
reciprocity. . . . [These lessons] teach surely one thing
above all—a need for extreme caution, a sense of the
appalling vastness and complexity of the forces that can
be unleashed, and of the egg-shell delicacy of the
arrangements that can be upset.*

—Barbara Ward and René Dubos, 1972

1

One of the few differences that really dichotomize mankind is
the attitude toward surprise. The very young and the very old
love it (this is the link between them); so do the idle rich, the
scientist in his laboratory, and the artist secure in his craft. But
those who are responsible for the lives of others, in their work
or at home, must fear surprise, and often hate it. Even the

pleasant surprise is distrusted: a favorite newspaper story in all cultures tells of the lottery winner whose good fortune brings him nothing but trouble. There is supposed to be (I don't trust these things) a Chinese curse that wishes upon its victim the fate of living in interesting times; it expresses the rational man's rational fear of surprise.

Nevertheless, surprise is with us always. As David Hume pointed out more than two hundred years ago, the future is strictly uncertain; more recently, a Rand Corporation study proclaimed that regardless of the tools we create we will never be able to predict more than two weeks ahead something so foreordained as the weather. And, of course, a world completely without surprise would be intolerable. The most sober-sided divine, the most worry-wart mother, comes upon a day when every nerve end demands that something out of the ordinary must happen. The newspapers tell of the calamities that befall the lottery winner; but in one way or another everybody buys lottery tickets.

Saturation comes quickly. If our expectations are so far off the mark that we are frequently surprised, we feel a mounting, disappointed, irritated malaise. Alienation, the sociologists say; rootlessness; powerlessness. The words are so pronouncedly pejorative it is hard to remember that they describe the unalterable human condition. We are alienated because we live in our bloodstreams while pretending to a larger environment; rootless because time will not stand still; powerless because all we care about is forever at the mercy of a drunk driver or a wild cell. Uneasy lies the head that wears the crown. Those who told us it could be otherwise—and they were thick as flies in the 1960s—were cruel deceivers.

But not all the surprise we suffer is necessary. The individual is a cork on the sea, but in broad outlines what happens to a community should be mostly predictable most of the time. Hume's example of strict uncertainty, after all, was the lack of a guarantee that the sun will rise tomorrow; but not many of us would hesitate to bet on that. The reason people become upset

—or so we are told—is that their view of stability is pre-Newtonian. They expect the world to stay the same, which cannot be, and do not understand that a truly stable world is one in which everything stays in motion at the same speed in the same direction. Thus they become the victims of what their betters, busy envisioning the society of the year 2000, labeled "future shock."

Unfortunately, the expectations of the sophisticated have in recent years turned out to be even farther off the mark than those of the people they presume to instruct. That sort of error reverberates: we call it a "failure of leadership."

2

The reasons we were misled in the 1960s are many and various and of varied importance. Some of the trends that were taken as fundamental were in fact superficial: juvenile rebellion and the ingestion of psychotomimetic drugs, to take the most obvious. Some were merely phases in what should have been recognized as a repetitive cycle—in the birthrate, for example, or the acceptance of licentiousness in the arts and public behavior, or the rapidity of economic growth, or the degree of concern for the civil liberties and civil rights of individuals. And where the forces considered were indeed fundamental and progressive rather than cyclical (technological change, for example, which is irreversible barring catastrophe), the analysts of the 1960s ignored Garret Hardin's biologist's warning "You can never do just one thing." Newtonian projections assume a world without friction or limits, and we have both. All trend lines peter out somewhere, or meet obstacles, and events force redirection.

The early 1960s were a time when the leadership of American society fell into the hands of the intellectual community. There was faith in planning regardless of the quality of the information on which the plans were made; faith, rather than mankind's long-standing and well-founded distrust, in government; faith in education and the malleability of democratic man. Slogans never capable of supporting much more than hope were reified by academics and lawyers working in symbiosis: nondiscrimination became equal opportunity became affirmative action became goals became quotas became "equality of outcomes." A "war against poverty" would eliminate "the causes of crime"; doctrines of love or of permanent revolution would create a "new man" who would learn without the vulgar calculus of reward and punishment. Banker John Bunting declared that depressions were "against the law"; economist Walter Heller argued that even recessions could be prevented by "fine-tuning." On the dizziest heights of intellectual fashion, the capacity to postpone gratification was seen as the curse rather than, as Jacob Bronowski almost alone insisted, the glory of civilization. (For Bronowski the capacity to postpone gratification makes possible not just civilization but *man:* the act of "keeping tools for future use" was the "lunge into technological foresight" that "released the brake on evolution.")

Most disturbing was the reluctance of the planners to learn from the experience of those who carried out their proposals. Program Planning Budgeting Systems were being pushed onto governmental bodies long after it had become clear that the information necessary to make such procedures work effectively was nowhere to be found. At a meeting of the American Assembly in 1968, when the first generation of TFX fighter-bombers were falling like flies on their test flights, Senator John McClellan was still being ridiculed for his failure to understand that the Defense Department's decision about how to build the damned thing had been derived from systems analysis and therefore had to be correct. In December 1974, with unintended irony, the business section of the *New York Times* printed on the same page a John Kenneth Galbraith speech proclaiming that in the future governments would have to plan economic activity in great detail and a letter from the head of the National Bureau of Economic Research complaining that in early fall 1974 it was impossible to give even the most general guidance to government policy because the important statistical indicators were yielding contradictory information.

"There is no learning," said psychologist Edward Thorndike, "without knowledge of results." It turns out to be a necessary but not a sufficient condition. Left to their own devices, academics may concentrate their attention on superficial trends and extrapolate from them recklessly, whatever the emerging results. Businessmen who make mistakes lose money and look for something else to do; academics who make mistakes find that their research has produced "insufficient evidence." They seem to be led astray by the search for subtlety. Their disciplines penetrate corners of the world through techniques that begin with the exclusion of everything not to be found in these corners. Because the process of definition necessary to academic study makes the subject under study so amenable to control, the academician comes to see the world as far more submissive to policy than it is.

How good everything was going to be, back in the 1960s, now that the philosopher-kings were in charge! At the Harvard University Program on Technology and Science (now discontinued), director Emanuel Mesthene saw "genuinely clean cities and genuinely clean governments; truly universal literacy; eradication of hunger and disease; real brotherhood of the more and less favored; and common progress toward human dignity by direct example and transfer of skills. . . . The ideals are as sound as they are classic. Accomplishment has fallen short in the past because they have been uneconomical."

With such targets in our sights, we became subject to the influence of the "Fourth Law" propounded by the maverick sociologist Marion Levy—that "good intentions randomize behavior." The hubris of American experience acquired intellectual resonance. We began to believe that our proposed policies would have to work because the outcomes would be so attractive; slowly, slowly but in the end all but irrevocably both government and business fell into the habit of legislating (or planning) outcomes. "If we can put a man on the moon . . ." No soap.

Everything we do influences our future; but nothing we can do will control it. Believing we can control the future, we grow unprepared for surprise, and we lack ideas about what to do next when the plans go wrong. Poor Mesthene! It would be his fate to become president of one of the satellite colleges established in a New Jersey urban slum by Rutgers University, and to be subjected to a sit-in by sixty angry and frightened students when he proposed that college diplomas should be awarded only to those who could pass a basic literacy test.

3

Let me pause here for three extended examples of plans that are certain to go wrong and produce unpleasant surprises, because their authors believed they could legislate results, forgetting that what actually happens is influenced more by people's real interests and underlying drives than by the words of a law or by publicized fashion. All three mistakes were made with such high purpose that it is almost an act of bad manners to point out that the policies adopted or proposed run counter to what people want or expect from their society and are therefore doomed to disappointment.

First, *an error of technique:* the Clean Air Act of 1970.

The conditions the act seeks to remedy are, Lord knows, real enough; nobody who travels by air can have failed to notice the plumes of filth that rise from American cities. But behind the law lay an unstated major assumption: that technology could be created by fiat—that an effective, inexpensive technique for cleaning up emissions from automobile tailpipes and power plant smokestacks would be brought into existence within five years if the law in its majesty so required. This assumption was false. The efficiency of standard-sized American cars dropped drastically from the 1972 to the 1974 model years: the new cars were hard to start in cold weather, stalled easily, and could travel only a little more than half as far as the 1972 cars on the same tank of gas. (Official figures from the Environmental Protection Agency showed a drop of only 20 percent in fuel economy; but the experience of drivers on the road did not bear out the announced results of the EPA tests.)

Automobile manufacturers, then, were compelled by law to offer to the public cars of a lower performance quality than those the same public had bought in previous years. Now, it is part of the genial folklore of American social criticism that mass production and standardization reduce quality; people put up with it, the folklore says, because those awful monopoly capitalists have deprived them of choice. But the wellsprings of consumerism have been the constant improvement in the performance and indeed the durability of mass-produced merchandise. It is simply taken for granted that new models of anything—cars, refrigerators, washing machines, television sets, calculators, houses, artificial fibers, medicines—will be "better" than the models they replace. In fact, thanks to the widespread introduction of electronic ignition systems, the 1973-model cars were mostly better than the similar 1972-model cars, despite certain items of added weight (impact-resistant bumpers, etc.) required by new government safety regulations. But the 1974 models were dramatically "worse."

Admittedly, the decline in quality came at an unlucky time. The extra costs of pollution-control and safety equipment had to be loaded atop the price increases of a mounting inflation, and the Organization of Petroleum Exporting Countries was about to push the price of oil to unbearable levels. Meanwhile, four years of litigation by the Sierra Club and the Friends of the Earth had made it impossible to build the pipeline that would otherwise have carried Alaskan oil to mainland America by 1973. (To have had another 1.5 million barrels a day of domestic oil available in 1975 would have been worth $5 billion a year to the United States at the going world price; but the real value would have been much greater. Total imports of Arab oil to the United States ran only 1.3 million barrels a day in spring 1975.) Carrying out another mandate of the Act, officious young lawyers in the EPA's regional offices nailed down the lid on the coffin they had designed for the nation's cities by demanding reductions in the number of downtown parking spaces sufficient to force both shoppers and employers out of the urban centers. In Los Angeles, EPA mandated an 82 percent reduction in the use of automobiles; thereafter, presumably, the nation would find other sources for the goods Los Angeles factories used to produce, and would appropriate the funds to make it possible for half the families in Los Angeles to survive after the breadwinner lost his job.

The new regulations and the drumfire of attacks on the automobile that accompanied them did unquestionably hold down the sales of cars, but they may not have significantly advanced the cause. When Congress repealed the requirement for a seat-belt interlock, which had jiggered the 1974 cars in such a way that they would not start until both occupants of the front seats had fastened their belts (if then), it was admitted that this feature had been stripped by garage mechanics from at least three-fifths of the cars compelled to provide it; and the 1974 emission-control equipment was similarly sabotaged by many owners—especially as the price of gasoline went up. (If the administration had imposed gasoline rationing, or a very steep tax on gasoline at the pump, even more cars would have been tuned in ways that improved mileage at the price of increased emissions.) Cities refused to draw up plans for suicide, and courts refused to compel them to do so. Most important of all, people whose old cars were still operating reasonably well refused to buy the new ones. The road to recession was opened up by the decline in automobile sales in fall 1973. The air did not get much cleaner; transportation costs rose dramatically; and the unemployment rolls were much longer than they would have been in the absence of the Clean Air Act.

The basic error here was the insistence that people would have to buy inferior cars if the government forbade the production of superior cars. They didn't have to, and they didn't. Prices of used cars rose even faster than the prices of new cars; in fall

1974, when the 1975 models with their catalytic converters offered purchasers something else that could go wrong, manufacturers advertised despairingly that for the man with an old car to trade the net price of a new car was actually less than it had been in the recent past. But even price rebates and price reductions could not bring automobile sales within 30 percent of the sales in 1972 and 1973 model years. A great deal of distasteful mendacity was forced upon all the public participants in discussions of the automobile market. Automobile manufacturers had to claim that the new cars were better, for they could not hope to sell them otherwise; consumerists who had environmental interests were forced to go along with the falsehoods of the manufacturers; and the Department of Labor in drawing up its cost-of-living indices had to deny the reality of the price increases in automobiles by taking the costs of the pollution-control and safety devices as "improvements" in the cars. (The costs of improvements wash out of the Consumer Price Index.) By the end of 1975, when it became apparent that full recovery in the economy could not be achieved as long as most automobile owners liked their present cars better than the new cars, the failure of the Clean Air Act was a center of major disturbance in American politics.

I call this a failure of technique, because I believe we could have got farther along the road to our objectives if we had gone about the business of government rather differently. The authors of the Clean Air Act could not know what emission standards were technically achievable, and could not intelligently estimate either side of the cost-benefit equation. (They still can't.) In laying down prescriptions, they guaranteed only that human ingenuity would be employed to circumvent unworkable rules. What might have been feasible was the imposition of an excise tax schedule based on both the chemical content of emissions and the efficiency of automobile and truck engines. Given the complicated bad luck of 1973–75, even the most carefully planned tax-incentive program could have failed (European car sales also declined, though not so severely as ours); but a law written with greater understanding of its consequences would have done less harm and might have done more good.

Manufacturers, instead of seeking ways to escape the rules, would have been plunged into competition to develop devices to avoid the tax. The cost increases required for improvement in air quality would have been offset by tax reductions; the costs imposed by dirty air would have been made palpable by tax penalties. The balance of costs and benefits would still have been subject to considerable control through the setting of tax rates—but the judgment of the values to be placed on the terms on both sides of the equation would have been determined by makers and customers (who are good at this sort of thing) rather than by bureaucrats (who are not). And Congress by temporarily reducing the emissions tax would have had a simple and efficacious way to stimulate demand for automobiles.

Next, *an error of social purpose:* the effort to promote "ethnicity" through bilingual education of little children.

Like the Clean Air Act, our promotion of ethnicity expresses sound instincts. Diversity is not only interesting, it is functional: alternate ways of doing something human have survival values for the species. Even for those of us who like the Middle American (and our name seems less than legion in the intellectual community), the visible diminution of ethnic and regional differences has been a sad spectacle.

But all the enduring trend lines in the modern world run strongly against ethnicity within a national culture. In America all ethnic groups watch the same television shows, live in boxes of similar design and decor, wear about the same clothing at equivalent outdoor temperatures, and eat the same damned convenience foods. Fifty years ago, none of that was true. The nationality-based social club and athletic team, the foreign-language newspaper, the church, the kosher butcher, and the ethnic political organization are all in steep decline—in most cases, terminal decline. The index of marriages across religious and ethnic (even racial) lines has been rising rapidly, and the residential patterns of today's suburbs are much less ghettoized than those of yesterday's cities.

No doubt the reality of the melting pot used to be overstated by its myth. Ancestry always played a role in most Americans' self-image, in their voting tendencies at election time, in the athletes whose triumphs they applauded, in the historical figures whose anniversaries they celebrated. As a boy in New York, I went to a Metropolitan Opera Sunday-night benefit farrago and was surrounded by Italians; to Randall's Island to watch Gunnar Haeg race Greg Rice, and was surrounded by Scandinavians; to Yankee Stadium to see Billy Conn fight, and was surrounded by Irishmen—and what I had in my closet back home was a baseball bat personally autographed, in my presence, by Hank Greenberg.

But during the last decade, just in time for the ethnicity revival, the myth has been made true by telecommunications, jet aircraft, nationally advertised brands and causes, corporate branch offices, and the pervasive federal bureaucracy that sets standards on everything from the acceptable preparation of country hams to the alcohol content of folk medicines. Age group, occupational specialty, and income stratum have become much more influential than ethnic background or geographical location in forming the tastes and attitudes of Americans. Only in situations where daily life is isolated from social reality—in jails, on college campuses, and on military bases—does ethnicity alone play more than a marginal role in determining the life-style of white English-speaking Americans. And even age, occupation, and income are frail barriers to the rush of cultural conformity. "The American community that is being talked of so often, and so profoundly," Roger Starr observes, "is essentially superficial and highly mobile. Provided only that a certain homogeneity of social class and income can be maintained, American communities can be disassembled and reconstituted about as readily as freight trains."

Similar forces are at work in all the wealthier countries. The differences between a Yorkshireman and a Cornishman, a

Bavarian and a Rhinelander, a Roman and a Milanese, a Burgundian and a Norman have all been severely diminished in the past fifty years. François Mauriac writes sadly that "we no longer think about that period when every province formed a world which spoke its own language and built its monuments, a refined and hierarchical society which was not aware of Paris and its fashions. Monstrous Paris, which fed on this wonderful material and exhausted it!" Everywhere, the urban encroaches on the rural, property and possessions spread their umbrellas of attitude over what were once proletarian communities, technology destroys craft, literary traditions (which include for this purpose film and television) overwhelm oral traditions. But all this is part of the wallpaper—as unremarkable as the water coming out of the tap when you turn the handle—and the attention goes elsewhere.

Daniel P. Moynihan and Nathan Glazer have found a plausible explanation for the recent stress on ethnicity: it reflected the ever-increasing role of government action in the allocation of economic rewards, and thus the value of forming a distinct and separate aggregation that can put forth a claim to largesse. They link ethnicity also to "the return of ascribed rather than achieved characteristics as determinants of social stratification." Benjamin Franklin had considered it the greatest of American accomplishments that on this continent a man was judged by what he could do rather than by what he was; today's self-proclaimed "radicals" demand that if people are to be judged at all it must be by what they are rather than by what they can do. What you are, without reference to what you can do, must reduce to the fact of being somebody's child.

The arrangements Moynihan and Glazer describe are functional for ethnic leaders—whose own community is no longer willing to pay for their support—and for sweatshop operators because isolated communities are the most easily exploited, but not for anybody else. The allocation of economic rewards without reference to economic contribution is a luxurious inefficiency, which can be seriously proposed and generally tolerated only in very rich countries, and then only in the euphoric economy that characterizes the very top of the business cycle. In the recession of 1975, the tide of purely ethnic concerns ran out very rapidly.

But it left a great deal of muck behind—most notably, bilingualism in the schools, which publisher William Jovanovich has accurately described as "liberalism gone mushy, a tolerant conviction that everyone has a right to be handicapped." As can be demonstrated by the agonies of Belgium, India, Nigeria, and Yugoslavia, the malaise of Swedish Finland, Tyrolese Italy, and French Switzerland and French Canada, bilingualism is nonfunctional in the daily working lives of people whose incomes and satisfactions derive from things rather than from ideas, which means most people. Studies by the Columbia University manpower project show that away from New York City, in places where they grow up in an exclusively English-speaking setting, mainland-born Puerto Ricans earn average incomes almost equal to those of the general population (and two-thirds of them, by the way, marry non-Puerto Ricans). Inside New York City, where they grow up in Spanish-speaking enclaves, mainland-born Puerto Ricans earn substantially less average income (and only one-third marry non-Puerto Ricans).

Among the more prominent grounds for self-congratulation at the dedication ceremonies for the new College of Education building at the University of New Mexico in 1964 was the final elimination of a long-established bilingual primary school program that had produced "children illiterate in two languages." The idea that the federal courts and the Congress would force the restoration of this viciously discriminatory system would have been unbelievable then, and will soon be unbelievable again; but for a while we are stuck with it. Ethnic leaders will be kept happy today, and the children will pay for it tomorrow.

Third, *an error of analysis:* the campaign for rapid rail transit as the mass transportation of the future.

Like ethnicity, rail transit is the wave of the past: the trolley car and the "interurban railroad" flourished in the period 1890–

1925. In the first decade of the century, there were more than thirty thousand miles of such track in the nation's cities and suburbs. Rail transit made possible the growth of the American city. It moved faster than the horse, made less mess, and in an age when there was cheap labor to build and maintain the rail line and operate the trains, its costs were low. It did blight neighborhoods (good homes were rarely found near the railroad tracks or beside the el, and the avenues where the trolleys ran were or became predominantly commercial), and to function efficiently it demanded considerable density of settlement along the skeleton of the route map. But there was no choice.

Despite the anachronistic concern about overcrowding that was common in psychological literature of the 1960s, American cities are much less densely settled today. Factories, shopping centers, movie theaters, and increasingly office buildings scatter around the periphery, denying to rail transit the focal points necessary to make fixed corridors financially viable. In the American city of the future, obviously, "downtown" is going to be only one of many nodules of development—with luck, the biggest and the best, providing commercial and cultural magnets that make for a more cosmopolitan center city; but even then, no more than *primus inter pares*. Such a city will not generate the narrow corridors of traffic rail transit requires.

Construction and maintenance of rail lines, moreover, are horrendously expensive at modern wage rates. Because rail cars are much heavier than automobiles (or buses) and rest all their weight on a few square inches of wheel surface, rail beds require much more care and attention than highways. There are great numbers of people to be paid to do chores the car-owning family does for itself. And except for those who live very near one stop and work very near another, cars get their owners from home to job considerably faster than rail transit.

Electric rail is *not* energy-efficient. "Transit," writes Boris Pushkarev of the New York Regional Plan Association, "wastes two-thirds of the fuel in the process of converting it into electricity." Even at the present low level of occupancy per car, automobiles as efficient as the average foreign car burn little if any more fuel per passenger-mile when compared with consumption per passenger-mile by electric rail transit. The air pollution generated by fossil fuel power plants for railroads and subways would be almost as great as that generated by the automobiles—though presumably the power plants could be located farther away from the people affected. On a public cost basis, the comparisons are frightening. A couple of years before BART opened in San Francisco, one of the authority's senior executives worked out its costs and demonstrated that giving a new Volkswagen every five years to every one of the forty thousand or so daily users of the rail system would be cheaper than paying the operating, interest, and amortization costs BART would incur over and above its receipts. To make all the residents of the Bay Area pay a sales tax to subsidize rail transit for forty thousand (most of them suburbanites) seemed to me then and seems to me now a peculiar example of social justice. And the maximum hoped-for reduction in Bay Area car use from this huge subsidy was roughly 1 percent.

I am a New Yorker born, bred, and resident, and a user of public transit on most days of the week; and I believe in it (especially as a way to raise children, who are much better off if they can get where they want to go by boarding a subway or a public bus and are not slaves of a school bus schedule or a mother's willingness to drive the car). And I agree that there is an element of madness, and distasteful wastefulness, about the current American commuter system that sends millions of men and women from home to work and back each day, one to a car. Urban transportation in the future will almost undoubtedly involve a greater reliance on buses, and on minibuses or jitneys that carry people in small groups, door to door. But rail transit can never again be more than a minor factor: rail transit is the mobility of the immobile, and for better or worse America is used to moving around.

If the rail system were now in being, it could be argued that heavy taxation of automobiles and heavy subsidy of rail use could turn the trend around. I suspect that the argument is false (the opening of two new large-scale rail lines down the center dividers of the Chicago freeways, where during rush hour stalled drivers could watch the rail cars whiz by, did not reverse the declining use of Chicago's transit system), and in present circumstances it is irrelevant. The rail lines are not in being, and it takes twenty years to build them. By then, the corridors they occupy—permanently—will no longer exhibit the traffic patterns that made rail transit seem plausible to editorial writers and political leaders today. Roads are much more flexible: it is easy to build new feeder roads to serve highways as patterns of land use alter. And we have not even looked at the value to be placed on the comfort and the sense of personal safety and inviolability people feel in their cars as against the crowding and the danger they sense in crime-afflicted subways—or the convenience of getting in one's car and going on one's own schedule without the nuisance of planning every move according to a timetable.

But in the American 1970s, rail transit has acquired among opinion leaders a status comparable to that of the cow in India. In the agony of New York City, amidst all the keening over the waste of money during the last decade, nobody even mentioned the hundreds of millions of dollars just sunk into digging a hole under Second Avenue for a subway that certainly will not be running before the 1990s, and probably will never run at all.

4

As it happens, I believe in paying a high price to reduce air pollution, in cultivating all the group differences that can be saved, and even in the extension of public (if not rail) transit systems. I also believe that free markets following the paths of least current cost (which is what free markets tend to do) will not achieve unaided the feasible goals most of the country legitimately wants to reach: there is an important place for political decision over and above the entertainment value of politics.

Political decision has always been significant, for good or ill, only to the extent that it answers questions posed by the development of a society. Britain would not have become so dominant industrially without the repeal of tariffs on grain, which allowed the swelling cities to be fed on cheap imports from America and the Baltic (and sped the exodus of the yeoman farmer to the industrial city). France would have challenged Britain more effectively except for its retention of high tariffs on grain, which kept the peasants on the farms. Rich Uruguay stagnated economically and grew poor in the aftermath of social legislation that encouraged people to retire and become unproductive at the age of fifty; poor Japan waxed industrially mighty on the decision to provide only a minimum of public social services, forcing people to save for the education of their children and for possible misfortune (meanwhile promoting private savings by delivering a large portion of people's wages and salaries in two annual bonus chunks rather than week by week). The American suburb grew so fast and so far thanks in large part to fertilization from government subsidy of road construction, federal mortgage insurance, and tax exemptions for mortgage interest and local taxes.

What counts in the world is not what you hope to achieve but what does in fact happen. Our three errors result from setting public policy athwart the trend lines of the society, seeking to block rather than to direct the desires of the people who will be affected. We attempt these impossibilities because we have lost our sense of the difference between "issues" and realities: we have created for ourselves, because it is simpler, a *politique* of myths and power fantasies. We have grown dangerously like the child in the ill-taught math class who cannot see why the sailboat should not be traveling at 1,713 miles an hour.

"A writer may, to be sure, make any hypotheses he pleases," Robert Malthus wrote sternly to David Ricardo nearly 160 years ago; "but if he supposes what is not at all true practically, he precludes himself from drawing any practical inferences from his hypotheses." Our intellectual inheritance is pragmatism, and we must preserve and nourish it, because the straightforward consideration of consequences is still what we do best. Today's pessimism is at least as unjustified as yesterday's optimism, even less functional, and even more vulgar.

Looking forward, we do not have to be surprised as often as we are.

2

Four Forces

If we could first know where we are, and whither we are tending, we could better judge what to do, and do it better.

—*Abraham Lincoln*

1

In the first chapter, we considered three "tendencies" that could be disregarded by policy-makers—government officials or businessmen—only at peril to their policies. All three are in fact rather deep-seated: the spirit of progress as expressed in the constant improvement of consumer goods, cultural homogenization, and the search for increased privacy expressed as a preference for individual rather than "mass" transit. Drawing up a list of tendencies, however, is an ultimately fruitless occupation, because what will be left out is at least arguably more important than what is included, and because tendencies are essentially phenomena; they require almost as much explanation as they supply. What we need if we are to look ahead with some decent probability of accuracy are tendencies deep enough in the history of our society and wide enough in their effects to be considered "forces."

I shall be arguing that the parameters within which we live as a community have been set for the last quarter of a century by the working out of four such forces, and barring nuclear catastrophe the same four forces are all but certain to dominate the continuing development of American and European society in the next quarter of a century. One cannot, of course, constrain complicated societies within a simple construct of four forces, and every attempt to explain human behavior involves what the economist R. W. Clower has called "delusions of competence." So be it. The argument here is that explanations or extrapolations that do not take account of this quadrumvirate should be distrusted—and that the more closely an explanation or prediction can be tied to these forces, the more likely it is to be true. All four are already part of our background knowledge, of course: indeed, one of the reasons for our failure to use them analytically is that they bore us: we already know about that: what's new? But what's new is still in the womb of something older.

The four forces are as follows:

1. The vast increase in national product and wealth.
2. The rapid growth and refinement of technology, and its differential impact on different areas of human endeavor.
3. The diminishing effectiveness of the social mechanisms by which individual choices are organized into apparently institutional decisions.
4. Population trends.

Seriatim, now:

2

1. The vast increase in national product and wealth. We have in fact, as the economists at the beginning of the century predicted, performed the magic of compound interest—the application of a relatively steady growth rate to an ever-enlarging base.

Between 1950 and 1973, the income of the average American family rose by something like 80 percent, in real terms—

that is, after allowing for inflation. The increase alone in the real American national product in the three years 1971–73—again, after allowing for inflation—was more than half as great as the entire American national product in 1937. This is like astronomy: we simply cannot comprehend the distances.

In 1937, America produced 2.2 million cars, and imported none; in the 1973 model year, America produced just under 10 million cars, and imported about 1.4 million more. In 1937, one household in every fifteen acquired a new car; in 1973, it was almost one in five. In 1937, per capita consumption of beef in the United States ran about 64 pounds a year; in 1973, it was 120 pounds. And 1937 was *not* a depression year: it was the year we thought we had finally got out of the depression (1938 taught us better), the year our national product in constant prices climbed back above the 1929 figure.

The prosperity of 1972–73 was, of course, too much. In the first quarter of 1973, the American economy was growing at a rate of 8 1/2 percent per annum on an already gigantic base, and such growth rates are not sustainable. Though the Arabs and the ecologists have been no help, the fact is that today's deep recession was made necessary by the overblown prosperity of 1972–73, and would have occurred if neither Faisal nor Russell Train had ever been born. In the United States, the gross national product in real terms has been growing at almost 4 percent a year for more than a quarter of a century, averaging out the good years and the bad years. This sort of secular trend has a momentum of its own: unless the ratio of savings to consumption changes drastically, bursts of faster growth must be paid for by recession, which in turn establishes the preconditions for accelerating growth, until the lines of actual growth again intersect the historic trend.

Resumption of the established growth trend will be made more difficult by the energy cartel and the ideologists of the environment, but ways will be found to cheat the sheikhs and befuddle the ecologists. For five centuries, urban intelligence, the spirit of the free and productive towns, has created and taken a steadily increasing share of the world's output. It is certainly possible (anything is possible) that our steps have taken us to the watershed, that in the years ahead wealth will run back to what Marx (anticipating the Third World) labeled "rural idiocy." But the real shortages in the world are still organizing ability and insight, not petroleum and protein, and the momentum of five centuries is not so easily turned aside.

The effects of affluence pervade our society. We are incredibly more healthy and free from physical pain; the most modest of us command resources of energy external to ourselves that would have astonished an ancient potentate; we routinely, rather grumblingly, satisfy wants that human animals of previous generations never knew they had. Where almost half the American population lived in officially categorized "substandard housing" in 1940—and almost two-fifths was officially ill-housed in 1950—less than 10 percent were so housed in 1970 and by 1973 the figure was probably 5 percent. In 1974, well over half of all American households had two or more television sets, and nearly two-fifths had two or more cars. Fully half of each age cohort was proceeding to some form of higher education, a luxury that had been available to only one-sixth of the nation's adolescents a generation before.

Culturally, the impact of our riches is overwhelming. The vast majority of the population easily takes care of its physical needs at these income levels, and the expenditure of most of the annual increase is discretionary. Popular taste commands ever-increasing purchasing power. Within limits to be looked at later, high culture flourishes—but its relative importance in the society declines because the increase in revenues available to popular culture is so much greater. To take a field I know well, the total money spent on recordings of classical music just about doubled from the mid-1950s to the mid-1970s, but such records became steadily less significant in the plans of recording companies because the money spent on popular music rose by a factor of five. The Chicago Symphony sells out at Carnegie Hall; but Alice Cooper sells out Madison Square Garden. When only the richer half of the country has a television set, network time will be allocated to a *Playhouse 90;* as soon as everybody has one, the network devotes itself to *Beverly Hillbillies* or *Mission: Impossible.*

The result is a pervasive feeling of democratization, or vulgarization, depending on one's mood. In print, this phenomenon goes back the better part of a century: the spread of literacy created the penny press and the dime novel, "yellow journalism" rather than Periclean exposition—though it also, on a smaller but not trivial scale, created the Haldeman-Julius blue books and the workers' education movement. There is also a striking public preoccupation with sex, which was always true of working-class entertainment (viz., George Orwell's essay on seaside postcards). Increasing income generates more and more open production and consumption of what was wanted before, not a change in tastes.

An increasing proportion of the community gains access to places and pleasures once reserved for their betters, and the established (and even new) rich begin wondering audibly about the dangers of crowding and "the quality of life." Franklin Roosevelt once told a charming story about the little boy who did not raise his hand when the teacher asked the class who wanted to go to heaven; "Sure I want to go to heaven," he said when pressed on the matter; "but not with *these* guys." In general—almost invariably—people with more money take up more space. In the life of our cities, there is much less crowding than there was, and the average quality of that life (including the cleanliness of the air) is clearly much higher than ever before. But the exclusionist middle class (and it is almost the definition of the middle class that it excludes) feels itself crowded as more people join, and sees a declining quality of life because the beach is full of people, the highway crawls, there are too many on line in the restaurant or at the museum.

The rich and well-born normally have a pretty self-image. Poor societies find all men ultimately equal because they die, and are thus all contemptible by comparison to the eternal

Godhead ("What is man, that Thou art mindful of him?"); a rich society finds everyone equal in a right to self-esteem, which has always been the most important quality men have purchased with big money. I'm OK, saith the prophet; you're OK. In education everyone gets at least a gentleman's C; if a student obviously has failed to learn something, blame may not only be placed on *but accepted by* the school.

Widespread wealth has economic and political consequences. The growth in the proportion of the population that holds property creates an ever-stronger desire for security, and fosters attitudes of protection rather than initiative in both individuals and institutions. Considerations of risk come to dominate considerations of reward, and even radicalism comes to focus on deprivations of security, inadequate health care and old-age pensions, rather than on remaking the world. Proposing a new theory of justice, philosopher John Rawls took risk-aversion as the *basic* human drive.

In the economy, a rich, security-conscious society increasingly demands the assurance of debt instruments (bonds, insurance policies, bank accounts) rather than the risks of ownership, a tendency greatly enlarged in the United States by the operation of the tax laws that make interest payments deductible by debtors from the income that will be taxed. In 1950, two-thirds of the nation's industrial capacity was financed by risk capital and only one-third by borrowed money; in 1970, two-thirds of it had been built on debt. The theory of the firm (the economists' explanation of corporate behavior) is nowhere near sufficiently developed to allow us to predict in any detail what happens when producers become increasingly dependent on borrowed money, but it does seem obvious that their capacity to take risks, or to react boldly to surprise, must be diminished. And "growth" apparently for its own sake must become an increasingly significant objective, because larger gross revenues increase the cover—the security—for the repayment of debt instruments. There is no need to posit undefinable "power drives" to explain the American corporation's insistence on growth.

Political life tends to be dominated by a felt need for social control. Distant rewards are promised rather recklessly, because the future is far away and larger than life, like the rising moon. But decisions about risks are taken on shrinking time horizons, because accuracy in prediction can be achieved only over the short term—and the first demand on the businessman or bureaucrat or politician is the reduction of risk. Marriages cannot be celebrated without a Wassermann, oil wells cannot be drilled without an environmental impact statement, drugs cannot be marketed without certification that nobody could be harmed by taking them. Linotypists must be protected from the consequences of computer processes, dockers from containerization, railroad firemen from dieselization, plumbers from the invention of foolproof plastic pipe, plasterers from the improvement of wallboard. I'm all right, Jack . . . If an airplane falls or surgery fails, the airline or the surgeon must expect to be sued. The state reimburses the owners of property damaged in a hurricane. Bad luck becomes illegal. Trial and error is out as a means of learning, because error is impermissible—and certainly too dangerous to admit.

Wealth brings a wild growth of "entitlements" or "rights." Frederick Pollock wrote Holmes that all lawyers know "that life would be intolerable if every man insisted on his legal rights to the full." But the lawyers of a rich society cheerfully demand their clients' full portion of rights, whatever the costs in increased crime and reduced efficiency. "Justice" becomes a rallying cry, and even religious leaders forget that if everyone got justice few would 'scape whipping. We use the word so often we do not realize that we have no agreed definition for it. Professor Rawls considers actions just when and only when they produce benefits for the least fortunate members of the society. But this falls straight into Benjamin Cardozo's trap, that "when talking about justice, the quality we have in mind is charity." Much of the tension in an affluent society reflects the fact that there is never enough self-esteem to go around.

3

*2. The rapid growth and refinement of technology, and its
differential impact on different areas of human endeavor.*

Without forgetting the major roles played by inherited totem
and taboo—and by climate, and by the avarice of militarily
stronger neighbors—it can be said with some safety that Marx
was right, that the technology of production is the greatest
single force in determining the economic and social organization of a society. The stirrup, says Lynn White, created feudal-
ism: a mounted warrior with his feet in a stirrup could carry a
shattering lance that would dominate a battlefield, and the feudal system of service as payment for land tenure was the most
efficient way to assure the recruitment of knights. The invention of the camel saddle, says Richard Ellier, made the desert
nomad the conqueror of the imperial horseman, created the
caravan society, and actually brought about the abandonment
of the wheel in the Middle East.

From the time when the heavy plow made the bottomlands
of northern Europe agriculturally viable, and the horse collar
widened the circle of the farmer's mobility, technological developments have been the tidal waves of history. By the 1950s,
they seemed controlled and tamed, sources of business cycles
rather than of revolution; but in fact the forces involved had
grown more dictatorial than ever. Technology changed the
relative costs and benefits of muscles and machinery, then of
agricultural and industrial products, now of services and goods.

Of course, technology does not operate in a social vacuum;
necessity may be the mother of invention, but custom defines
necessity. Alfred Whitehead once speculated amusingly about
how different history might have been if the Romans had been
tea drinkers, and had spent as much time as the English watching steam shoot out the spout of a kettle. But the Romans (indeed, the Greeks) knew about steam power: they used it to close
heavy temple doors. Fernand Braudel reports that thirty years
after Newcomen invented the steam engine there was only one

such device in use in the British Isles. A reasonably accurate book about flammable gas (both natural gas and gas made from coal) was published in France as early as 1618, but the first gaslamps waited another two hundred years.

"Everything is technology," Braudel writes, but later he adds that "without the growth of the capitalist towns . . . technology would have been impotent." Once eating begins, the appetite grows hugely. A few men saw that nonmuscular sources of energy greatly increased the profitability of storing rather than expending resources—i.e., of "capital formation"—and in a time brief enough to earn the name revolution industrialization transformed all the institutions of Europe and America. Presently an ever-increasing division of labor forced the creation of institutions through which unrelated individuals' total dependence on each other could be expressed and depersonalized— retail distribution networks, hospitals, stock exchanges, police forces.

Profound and trivial, the pieces of technology interrelate: automobile, mass communication of advertising, refrigeration, supermarkets. Among the most fundamental human attitudes is the tilt to convenience, the output of least effort for identical (or comparable) results, honored in our aesthetics as grace or elegance, in our economy as efficiency or productivity. In ways varied beyond the possibility of description, and equally pervasive at home and at work, technology changes what we do and what we admire—and this in turn influences what we think and how we perform.

Though Henry Ford's assembly line has the reputation, it is now clear that historians will regard the application of high technology to agriculture as the great American contribution. Reapers and binders, harrows, barbed wire, cross-breeding and ultimately hybridization, fertilizers, insecticides, irrigation systems, animal feeds, the immense range of storage and packaging techniques—until less than 4 percent of the nation's work force can feed the whole country, to standards of nutrition never known before. Meanwhile, the rivers were diverted through dynamos, the oil drillers roamed the world, and in Chicago in 1942 Prometheus broke the bonds forever. It is now de rigueur to complain about "agribusiness" and there are reasons for real concern about the exhaustion of petroleum reserves and the polluting effects of chemical combustion and nuclear reaction; but if one is going to think seriously about the human condition it is the accomplishments and not the secondary consequences that must be stressed.

Ever-cheaper food and ever-cheaper energy have been the outstanding characteristics of the twentieth century, more important than all the wars or ideologies or revolutions. And the most important development of the 1960s now appears to have been the frustration of energy technology—a result, I suspect, of the exploitation of very low cost Arabian oil, which blunted the incentives to apply cleverness to this problem. Without much cleverness, after all, the cost of electricity in constant dollars (considering inflation) had decreased every year from 1946 though 1971. While one cannot expect scientists to invent economical energy on schedule, any more than one can expect them to perfect environmental controls on schedule, history does argue that the sharp rise in oil prices has created the conditions for the discovery of techniques to reduce our reliance on oil. If in fact we are now facing fundamental constraints on the capture of potential energy, the doom-sayers will be right and the central arguments of this book will be wrong.

It is also true that societies can decay through the loss of their drive to absorb and employ new technology. Economists have argued that the handwriting was on the wall to depict the relative futures of Germany and England as early as the 1880s, when the Germans adopted the Gilchrist Thomas process for refining phosphoric iron ores, and the British did not. Today a Socialist government in Britain rather sanctimoniously calls for greatly increased investment in industry while the labor unions that support it flatly refuse to permit the use of any technology that might reduce the number of man-hours worked for each unit of output . . . Significantly, perhaps, it took Americans longer than it should have to use the basic oxygen furnace developed in Austria in the 1950s; and now, notoriously, the French are in mid-course of major nuclear power development blocked in America by propagandists of fear exploiting the weaknesses of democratic decision-making. Affluence, as noted, promotes risk-aversion; risk-aversion and the exploitation of emerging technology are necessarily in conflict. "If you invented a new product called 'salt,' " an advertising man said irritably the other day, "they'd never let you sell it."

Despite these frictions, American enterprise is still employing new technology at a clip fast enough to produce little-understood conflicts between public and private decision. Greater penetration of machinery into the manufacturing process and the development of computer-controlled tools continue to reduce the cost of manufactured goods—but it has not been possible to apply technology to a significant degree in the delivery of many of the most important *services* in the society: government, education, medicine, law, religion, art. Though there is general political agreement that such services should be expanded and improved, the increase in their costs relative to the costs of manufactured goods drives their apparent price higher than any price people as private decision-makers are prepared to pay. The price of a year in college or a week in the hospital or of police and fire protection rises dramatically while the price of a color television set or a Thanksgiving turkey remains stable or declines. Because technology can be applied to different activities in different degrees, it imposes "priorities" in conflict with those that might be felt if comparative costs remained stable. This aspect of the force of technological change is central to the political and economic life of our time; we shall look at its significance in detail in Chapter 4.

Increasingly sophisticated technology requires that men and women learn to perform tasks most of the members of the society cannot understand at all. Mysteries every bit as strange as transubstantiation are performed daily by people who are not even supposed to have priestly vocations. It is here that supposed "alienation" takes its grip, as everyone finds himself dependent on other people's accomplishment of assignments more complicated than the results of the work.

Familiarity makes machinery less frightening—men who crossed themselves the first time they encountered a door operated by an electric eye now stretch out on the bed and operate the television set by remote control. But the mysteries performed by people, flesh and blood like oneself, are always to one degree or another disconcerting. Everything is much worse when the mystery workers insist, as professionals always do, that they alone are capable of judging the quality of the work performed.

As the accountability debates in education and the malpractice furor in medicine have demonstrated, professional performance is inescapably unpredictable, as judged by its results: one cannot "guarantee" a reading lesson or an appendectomy the way one can guarantee an automobile muffler. But in a rich society, accustomed to technological progress, hope not only springs eternal: it bites. Persistent hopes of eliminating the insecurity that results from dependence on unpredictable professional performance gives resonance to calls for "participation" —calls that show consumer dissatisfaction with the results of professional performance, not an actual desire to participate. The crowd and its surrogates in the press demand a voice in who shall be coach when the team loses, not when it wins.

The side effects of technological change are often extraordinary and unexpected: both the automobile and television, for example, by removing to a private realm activities once undertaken collectively, have been great promoters of human selfishness. But the most remarkable of side effects from technology is still ahead of us, as we adjust our lives to the presence of the computer. For reasons that may reflect natural selection in human experience or may lie deep in the electrochemical constitution of the brain, our thinking is a search for an equilibrium or a temporary stasis; much of our greatest progress in understanding the world has come through our increased efficiency when we employ mathematical equations in the conduct of thought processes. The computer requires thinking by flow chart rather than by equation: stability is seen as arbitrarily imposed rather than naturally achieved.

John Maynard Keynes once observed that he thought the special power of Isaac Newton's analyses derived from Newton's ability to concentrate on a problem not just for a few minutes at a time but for weeks on end. But simply thinking about a problem in its originally perceived terms is not, in fact, a useful technique—even for a Newton or a Keynes. What is meant, I think, is the ability to follow through long and detailed sequential chains of if/then reasoning, moving off the trunk to branching sequences of changed terms and then back onto it without ever losing the audit trail to the premise. At some point the brain rebels, lapses into nonsense or accepts at least for the time being some conclusion that brings equilibrium. For that moment of satisfaction we have the significant symbol of the light bulb going on over the thinker's head: the scene is illuminated; ratiocination has become perception. But what is perceived may be a magician's trick.

Programmed to undertake such labors, a computer can keep in its guts an all-but-infinite sequence, complete with repetitive loops and searches along branch lines. The power of the tool is not fully appreciated even by most of those who use it, let alone by the public at large. I am among those who believe that in the end the computer will save us—that microcomputers will improve our sensing capacities and thus our control of our environment and efficiency in energy use, while macrocomputers will enable us to make more intelligent choices in business and in public policy by considering a much greater range of plausible consequences of our actions. But we are not there yet—not by a long shot. The hardware is coming on line (a bonus from space exploration, which tolerated no mistakes), but we do not have the immense quantities of necessary information in machine-retrievable form, or the algorithms that would permit its significant sorting and projection even if we had it.

Worries about a computer-dominated future are many, inescapable, and valid. Among them is a reasoned fear of the mistakes we will make as we lose the corrective power of our common sense, the balance inherent in the search for stasis. And most students who have looked at the problem share the late Harry Kalven's fear that through the retrieval capacity of the machine "mankind will lose its benign capacity to forget." Our self-image, moreover, is very much that of the thinking reed, and the notion of machines that "think" better than we do is extraordinarily destructive. The fact that the machine is essentially stupid and can do only what it is programmed to do does not really help our vanity much, partly because it will be programmed by some terrifyingly bright people and partly because at the end of the process it will be better at its selected chores than they are. There is a pleasant cartoon of a man asking a computer, "Is there a God?," and the computer typing out the answer, "There is now."

4

3. The diminishing effectiveness of the social mechanisms by which individual choices are organized into apparently institutional decisions. We call this, colloquially, a "loss of authority."

This one will need a little time, because here we come up against verbal habits that dangerously inhibit our understanding. Decisions are not made *by* the market or *by* the government; they must be made by people, *in* a market or *in* a political process. In neither is it likely that a real decision affecting the lives of many—a price or a law—will precisely express the desires of any one participant. But the word "decision" implies an end to the argument, at least for now: this *is* the price, that *is* the law of the land.

What amplifies the decision and makes it "institutional" is the process of its accomplishment, and few possibilities so disturb the normal American as the idea that institutional processes will fall under the control of a single individual or enterprise. We have a fear of executive authority which is forever being beaten upon, like a drum; a debunking tradition; and an array of anti-trust laws and agencies. We need to believe that the price is set by a play of market forces larger than any organization or individual, that the law is passed by elected representatives exercising their independent judgment and not by bureaucrats responsible to a boss. It is the process, not the people working in it, and not the immediate results as perceived by affected individuals, that commands respect and obedience. Because the process survives, a decision will be accepted even by those who consider it unfair: one lives to fight another day. For the time being, the individual voluntarily takes what he can get and does more or less as he is told, partly because it's too much trouble to do otherwise, partly because the decision he dislikes has acquired authority through the means of its production.

These processes have been very sturdy in the democratic-capitalist world, mostly because it rarely makes much difference how any one question is answered. What will happen is really being determined in the workshops and the market-places, and the supposed great issues that disturb the tranquillity of the age are at bottom intellectual entertainments. But these patterns of behavior require a minimal stability in everyday life, in the society and in the household: for most individuals most of the time, it must not make too much difference which way any one decision goes. Technology and affluence (through the growth of "needs") multiply the elements of interdependence, and increase the number of questions to which the answers will make more difference to more people. Thus—I am not joking—the revolution in Portugal aborted when the government replaced American entertainment programming with Eastern European educational programming on the state-monopoly television service. Many people's lives were adversely affected by this decision, and they turned against a government which had deliberately diminished their enjoyment of life.

Historically, changes in military technology have been the most obvious source of disturbances affecting large populations. The domestication of the horse, the invention of the ocean-ranging warship, the development of aircraft and then of missiles have successively expanded the breadth and depth of cultural diffusion. The absorption of influences external to a society or a culture is still the prime creator of decision-demanding episodes where the answer does matter. We noted in the last chapter the varying results from the political decisions made by England and France confronted with the prospect of cheap grain imports in the nineteenth century. Today, decisions about what to do in response to distant developments quickly touch the lives of everyone in a society. What happens in the Persian Gulf influences automobile purchasing in Oklahoma City, where there are oil wells in people's backyards; a drought in the Soviet Union affects the price of a loaf of bread in a grocery in the shadow of a grain elevator in Minneapolis. No society has or can develop institutional process that handles external stimuli without deliberate decision; as the external stimuli multiply, the burden on institutions increases.

What is true for societies in the production and consumption of goods is true for individuals and families in the production and consumption of services. When a son no longer follows his father's occupation, the school becomes utter necessity; when middle-aged women hold jobs, strangers must care for the old and sick; when a home is part of a service package that includes water and sewage and electricity, transportation facilities, police and fire protection, education and health services, the question of what government does in the community becomes crucial to the vitality of the household. Increasingly, governmental decisions impinge upon private decisions, and impact upon market decisions—and there is a vast growth in the realm of possible conflict between the results of disparate decision-making processes. Such conflicts demean the processes, and threaten the integrity of the decisions. Constituencies rise up to support the specific decision, even at the expense of process,

when the decision has turned out wrong and properly functioning process would discard it.

Affluence and technology make it easier to resist acknowledg-
ing and correcting prior mistakes. Once upon a time, communities would settle in the flood plain; the year of high waters
would arrive, and the survivors would move elsewhere. Now
the government gets them out before they drown, reimburses
them for property losses, builds a more elaborate (but ultimately equally defective) flood-control project, and encourages
still greater settlement in areas where no one should live. We
have a word for our enlarged capacity to postpone the acknowl-
edgment of error: we call it "planning."

The rigidities show up most strikingly and most damagingly
in distortions of the economic marketplace, for the market is
necessarily the controlling institution in every society built—as
all modern societies are—on the division of labor. A market is
not just the best, it is the only rational way to allocate resources
in a developed economy. Even under socialism, as Oskar Lange
pointed out more than thirty years ago (and the Russians came
to realize about ten years ago), the efficient allocation of labor
and capital to competing needs requires at the least a simulated
market.

A market system is the only way participants in the society
can get all the information that enables them to know what to
do next. In the words of economist Clifton Wharton (president
of Michigan State University), "Price/cost signals are still the
most rapid socioeconomic communication device at the disposal of man for controlled and planned development. They
transmit their information more swiftly, more efficiently, and
more pervasively than any other system yet developed. Price/
cost signals carry information regarding what is wanted and
what is not wanted; who wants it and who is ready to pay for
it or to sell it; what is precious and what is not." In general,
obviously, low prices tend to increase demand and to restrict
supply by eliminating all producers who cannot meet their costs
at that price; high prices tend to restrict demand and increase

supply by luring new producers into the market or making it profitable for existing producers to add another shift or plant the back forty or what have you. Except in an economy of extreme scarcity, like that in China (if nothing is offered for sale but dull cotton pants and jackets, the output required from the clothing industry is highly predictable), it is simply not possible for a central authority to issue enough orders to tell everybody what to do—even on the far-out assumption that the central authority really knows enough to say what everybody ought to do.

Ralph Lapp asks who shall decide what part of the sub-bituminous coal we shall mine in the northern plains should go to power electric utility boilers and what part should be liquefied as gasoline. If this decision must be consciously made by a government agency, it can't be done—there would be study groups galore, congressionally mandated postponements, and at least six years would elapse before the Supreme Court disposed of the last challenges. The fuels market will make the choice automatically—no fuss, no feathers—and will make it tolerably near to "right." According to Lloyd Reynolds, even the Chinese have made significant use of price/cost signals to increase agricultural production: "prices paid by the state for farm products have been raised gradually, while prices paid by farmers have been stable or falling." The Chinese insist they don't *like* market mechanisms, but they pay people in cash money, not barter goods—and the recipients of the salaries then decide whether they want a watch or a bicycle, forcing the central planning unit to allocate resources to the watch factory or the bicycle factory according to relative sales.

The great advantage of decision-making in an economic market is that markets automatically, *routinely* force the recognition of error. Presumably, computers will someday make it possible for a bureaucratic society to recognize and correct mistakes; but this presumption is likely to remain just that, because bureaucracies are fundamentally motivated by fear of the discovery of error. If the American economy ran as the

Russian economy runs, Ford would still be making Edsels. Keynes once observed that man is rarely so harmlessly occupied as when making money, but the values of the market discipline are greater than that: greed is the *cleanest* of human vices, the one most easily rebuked by reality.

What is important about "free enterprise" is not the possibility of profit—which can easily be duplicated by state capitalism or socialism, as everyone who has dealt with Russian managers knows—but the possibility of loss. The freedom to be right, to cast the argument in its more familiar political science terms, is essentially worthless: only the freedom to be wrong is important. If no one is free to be wrong, the state (or the church), controlling the definition of right, controls at least the publicly uttered thought of all. But the freedom to be wrong will be generally acceptable to possible victims of error (especially if their own beliefs are passionately held) only when they know they can try again. It was not an accident that Justice Holmes used a marketplace analogy in his most eloquent defense of free speech: "When men have realized that time has upset many fighting faiths, they may come to believe . . . that the ultimate good desired is better reached by free trade in ideas—that the best test of truth is the power of the thought to get itself accepted in the competition of the market."

Unfortunately, nothing is that easy. The very fact that a market enforces losses provokes cheating by the participants: two hundred years have passed since Adam Smith noted that every social encounter of competitors quickly degenerates into a conspiracy to fix prices. It is difficult to develop institutional correctives when important activities—telephones and electric power service, to cite the most obvious—can be carried on only under monopoly conditions, by enterprises that the society cannot permit to fail, in circumstances where a uniform price must cover wildly disparate costs of providing the service to differently situated customers. Where very large investments must be made to enter the market (which is increasingly the case as technology develops) Wharton's "price/cost signals" may be ineffective in drawing new producers, because they cannot pay the entry fee. (This factor does not always control what happens, however: if the profit potential looks large enough, as it did in the 1960s in computers, the money will be found to finance a number of new producers even in fields where immense payments are required; and then most of them collapse and disappear.) Very large organizations, corporate or trade union as well as governmental, may avoid the recognition and correction of error for very long periods of time: every year Mayor Lindsay complained that New York's costs rose 15 percent while its income rose only 10 percent, but there was no mechanism to compel him to do anything about it. The market for professional services, because of the lack of performance measurements, is almost totally nonfunctional; the market for ideas can be dominated by sensation.

Markets have trouble with time horizons: that which is profitable today tends to be done even if the long-run implications are negative. Technology and spreading patterns of interdependence give greater persistence to marketplace as well as governmental decisions. And, of course, as Harvard law professor Milton Katz insists, the "cost" side of Wharton's "price/cost signals" is a function of a "legal order." The law makes the manufacturer pay for the land occupied by his factory but not for the air space occupied by the emissions from his smokestack. If he can spew foul water into the river and make the city downstream pay to clean it up, the real costs of his production are never assessed against his product, destroying the social value of the market signals that control his activities. Stripmined coal has been cheap because the shovel destroys the land (and the land around it) at no cost to the miner or his customer.

Examples of the failure of the legal order to assess costs grow progressively more subtle and complicated as technology advances, and may remain invisible even when they are important. One of the easiest waste products to recycle is the glass bottle, but the aluminum cap that became so popular in recent years leaves a thin ring of aluminum on the neck that fouls the glass-recovery process. What price convenience?—and without a change in the legal order, who is to pay it? Certainly, markets that produce decisions that disregard long-term consequences cannot be permitted to pile up what the newspapers call pollution and the economists call externalities.

Moreover, markets are less efficient in allocating capital than they are in allocating consumption goods. The essence of a properly functioning market is a difference in the participants' interests: the farmer has grown raspberries and his interest is to sell them at the highest price; the housewife knows her husband just loves raspberries and her interest is to buy them at the lowest price. Classical theory insists that if all participants in such markets are blessed with perfect information, a price will be set that exactly clears the market, high enough to exclude all those who at this price prefer money to raspberries (especially if strawberries are cheaper), low enough to prevent the farmers from making the kind of profits that induce increased supply. The essence of the situation is that the farmer must sell and the housewife is driven by family appetite to buy, and their different compulsions produce a price.

Improvements in technology, however, move more price setting to higher levels of abstraction, to financial markets where the real demands to be satisfied and the real goods to be produced are increasingly buried beneath paper blizzards. Financial markets are made by differences of opinion rather than by differences of interests; and where one opinion dominates, a market may cease to function. Perfect information will destroy a capital market. A high price on raspberries in the morning will reduce demand, and produce price cutting in the afternoon. But if the stock of a drug company goes up in the morning because there has been a patent application filed for a cancer cure, the odds are that the price will continue to rise in the afternoon: the price increases persuade new customers that this is a stock to buy while convincing possible sellers that if they hold on a while longer they will be able to sell for even more. Nobody in the situation *must* sell or buy: all purchases and sales express opinion about future prices rather than real interests.

Commodity futures markets, as a horrified government and citizenry learned in the summer of 1973 (and a horrified farming community and Third World learned in the winter of 1975), work the same way as stock markets. Millers buy wheat because they know they will need it to make flour—but if they believe wheat is going to be in short supply they may contract for future purchases of much more than they need, in the belief that they can later sell the contracts at a higher price level. And the public comes rolling in to buy and share the bonanza. These situations were always menacing: history records tulipmania and the South Sea Bubble, the stock market of 1929, and much else. As the technology for disseminating "information" improves, financial markets tend to oscillate more and more dramatically, because the tides of opinion reach farther up the backwaters.

Decisions made on the basis of price/cost signals—by governments, businesses, and individuals, in descending order of delay —take effect at some future time. When markets oscillate drastically, the actions resulting from a decision are likely to be out of phase with the needs of the society: that is, we will always tend to have too much or too little aluminum or hospital capacity, because the pots were added to the line or the beds purchased on the basis of information that reflected a speculative market swing or anticipated legislation rather than a true trend of demand. The textbook example is the cattle industry, because it takes so long to breed and raise and fatten a steer.

As society grows richer and more complicated, the ripples from disruptions of the market reach further into people's lives. Increasing division of labor creates increasing reliance on the market system for the performance of significant activities. Families once took care of their very old and very young at home, without reference to price/cost signals; now people pay, personally or through their taxes, for nursing homes and nursery schools. R. M. Titmuss, writing about the way blood donors behave and are recompensed in different cultures, stressed the significance of what he called "the gift relationship" in the cement of society. In a fully developed society where continuing division of labor is routine, the number and importance of these relationships relentlessly decline: we call the phenomenon "rootlessness." Moreover, as we shall see in Chapter 4, market valuation of what were once gift activities is much less generous than human feelings about them, and this dissonance between emotion and economics greatly distorts people's relations with their "community"—especially in times of inflation.

When a market fails to operate on appropriate time horizons, or allocates costs or rewards unintelligently, or punishes the public by protecting the powerful from the consequences of their mistakes, governments are pressed to "regulate." Obviously, much regulation is necessary, to secure honesty, competitiveness, and product safety; and as secondary consequences become more menacing, governments must redefine the legal order to enforce a more rational assessment of the costs of economic activity. But as technology and affluence increase people's belief that every problem has a solution, governments increasingly attempt to resolve particular market problems by particular solutions, often without help and sometimes against the grain of whatever automatic processes exist.

Once upon a time farmers decided, in a market context bedeviled by imperfect information, how much winter wheat they would plant. They usually planted a little too much, because, like everybody else, farmers are a bit greedy; and the result was steadily decreasing farm prices, pressures to get the crops up more efficiently, tendency toward deflation and—certainly in the 1890s and the early 1930s—depression. The government undertook to support farm prices and (a necessity if subsidy was to be less than infinite) to limit acreage and production. In fall 1972, with prices already up and the dimensions of the wheat deal with the Russians finally out in the open, the Department of Agriculture retained its restrictions on how much winter wheat should be planted. By late summer 1973 wheat was selling for more than three times its price in early summer 1972; by 1974 the worldwide food reserve available for the prevention of famine had disappeared.

By holding prices of domestic copper and fertilizer well below the world price, the Cost of Living Council inspired greatly increased exports of these (and many other) commodities, creating shortages at home. Twenty years of keeping a lid on natural gas prices gave false price/cost signals to both producers and users, encouraged worldwide flaring off of precious hydrocarbons, inadequate development of known and exploration for unknown resources, and overconsumption by low-priority users. In its full development, government regulation protects industry against change. When the first communications satellite went up over the Pacific, the Federal Communications Commission required its proprietors to charge much higher rates than they had planned, to preserve the profits of the companies that had laid the existing transpacific cables. Such procedures have been polished at the Interstate Commerce Commission to such a fine perfection that a disgusted midwestern trucker, blocked by railroad objections from reducing any of his shipping rates, filed a proposed tariff for the carriage of yak fat from Chicago to Omaha—and was indeed enjoined from putting this new tariff into effect after a formal objection from a law firm hired by the railroads to oppose everything any trucker requested from the commission.

Allan Meltzer has argued that today in the American economy as a whole "inappropriate public policies, not changes in private expenditures, become the main cause of instability." Government decisions tend to be incommensurate with market decisions: instead of changes at the margin, reflecting shifts of taste and preference expressed in price/cost signals, government offers a rule of law which proscribes and prescribes. Worse: people will vote for candidates who campaign for more integrated housing or cleaner air or more effective schools—but they won't live in a neighborhood with public housing projects, or buy the less efficient car, or pay the taxes for smaller classes. In the real world, limited resources impose choices; in the world of government, everyone can play Let's Pretend.

What is most disturbing is that destabilizing activities by governments are almost always carried forward in the name of stability itself, price controls and environmental controls being the obvious examples. Governments are no better than markets —maybe worse—in choosing appropriate time limits over which to measure the costs and benefits of their actions. And democratic governments may be crippled in making these decisions because future generations do not vote for present politicians.

Urbanization further weakens the capacity of a democracy to look ahead: unlike the farmer, who works his fields in rotation and plants windbreaks that may not mature until he is dead, urban man finds it hard to think on a high time horizon. "What is the City but the People?" was the title of New York's (now abandoned) Master Plan; but unless the city is seen as a *place*, the unborn generations who must live in it later will be sacrificed (as they have been, so obviously, in New York) to the transient interests of the merely living.

This exclusive concern for immediate impact is even extended to historical analysis. Barbara Ward and René Dubos in their background paper for the Stockholm Conference on the Human Environment wrote in 1972 that "the ruthless Baron Haussmann, carving out his celebrated boulevards in Paris, scattered the dispossessed poor to garrets in nearby slums, greatly increased the density of population and with it the ravages of tuberculosis. . . ." Yet surely, more than a hundred years later, we can afford to give the ruthless Baron some credit for the invention of the Paris (the parks and squares as well as the boulevards) that has given so much joy to so many. To build New York's Central Park, Olmsted had to evict an army of squatters, the poorest of the poor; is there really anyone such an ass that he now regrets what Olmsted did? Attempts to rebuild the Woodlawn section of Chicago were stopped in the 1960s by the cry that "urban renewal means Negro removal" —but the benefits of vitalizing the political life of Woodlawn were much less widely shared than the benefits that would have resulted from even the most insensitive efforts to restore its physical amenities. Anyone who doubts it need merely visit the place. Once.

This said, it must also be said that a longer time focus sometimes calls into question the benefits of decisions that seemed reasonable, stable, even triumphant out to the limits of the time we can confidently predict. The insured self-amortizing mortgage, tax deductions for interest payments and local taxes, subsidies for highway construction—these social inventions of the 1930s, unquestioningly acclaimed for thirty years, can now be seen as creators of the conditions for the decay of our cities in the 1970s. Environmental protection itself may be a two-edged sword: the harm done to northwestern timberland by the infestation of the tussock moth through two long years when the EPA forbade spraying with DDT may be entirely comparable to the harm done by strip-miners to the valleys of Appalachia; and the catalytic converters (like the nuclear tests) are introducing to our atmosphere new poisons with which we have had no experience whatever.

In the next few decades men will have to take what Lincoln Gordon calls "a growing class of strategic and often irreversible decisions," and right now there can be few subjects of study more important than the history of the great improvement projects. What was on the minds of the Chinese who planned the canal from the Yellow to the Yangtze? or the Italian peasants who first terraced Umbria? Remember the Mesopotamians whose water and irrigation systems in the end destroyed the civilization that created them, in a process to which we can now see ghastly parallels in Pakistan. The Aswan Dam has spread schistosomiasis among Egyptian farmers and destroyed the fresh-water fishing fleet at the mouth of the Nile. What is in the minds of the Soviet planners who are designing a project to divert Siberian rivers from their established Arctic destination to a southerly course? The global climatic consequences of a decrease in the supply of fresh water to the Arctic Sea look worse and worse as non-Russian scientists make their simulations.

A chemical spilled into the Rhine in Germany kills fish in Holland; damming the Colorado, Americans create saline irrigation water in Mexico; overfishing by the Japanese in the northern Pacific decimates the Columbia River salmon; Chinese nuclear tests poison the milk in Japan. Noel Mostert insists that oil from tanker accidents will kill the plankton in the southern seas, and there go all the fishes; various publications and citizen groups see the ozone vanishing before the onslaught of rising freon from aerosol cans, and everybody gets skin cancer from the unimpeded ultraviolet rays. No doubt much of this stuff is fantasy; but the governance problem is real.

I misuse the language, of course, when I describe as "a force" the decline of authority and competence in the decision-making institutions; it is a product of the affluence and technology vectors, and the expectations associated with them. Still, the effects are pervasive, and act to amplify other trends; and they must be dealt with in a separate context. They will be a preoccupation of this book. In the last chapters, I shall try to present some approaches to decision-making that might turn the trend line, and a few specific mechanisms to tide us over until we know how to do better—but I shall be offering them with a certain diffidence. We need lots of people thinking these things through in their own ways before we can renew confidence in our institutions. Even then, it will still be true, as Justice Holmes put it more than half a century ago, that "certainty generally is an illusion, and repose is not the destiny of man."

5

4. *Population trends.* We deal here, fortunately, with cyclical motion rather than with steady growth rates, at least in the United States and Europe. We deal also with a mystery: nobody really knows or even has any very good ideas why the popula-

tion of France was greater than that of Britain and Germany together at the time of Napoleon but less than that of Germany alone by the time of Clemenceau. The brute facts, however, are dazzling. From 1890 to 1960, the total increase in the American population between the ages of fourteen and twenty-four was 12.5 million. Then, in the one decade of 1960–69, that age cohort grew by 13.8 million. Obviously, there are many forces making life chances and attitudes different from generation to generation. But to talk of "generation gaps" (or the problems of education) without reference to demographic waves is as stupid as—well, as stupid as talking about "women's lib" without reference to the fact that in 1940 about 16 percent of the nation's females over twenty were spinsters, while in the 1960s the proportion had dropped to about 8 percent.

More subtly, the great jump in the size of the arriving age cohorts produced political and economic attitudes and habits that would not fit a less expansive age. It seemed more reasonable then to slough off onto the future the costs being incurred for present pleasures and present adventures, whether they took the form of atmospheric pollutants, pension commitments, or debt schedules. As the birthrate turned, a conservation ethic and a conservative politics rose together, and inflation enforced the lesson that the present cannot really compel the future to do anything at all. We are left with the great accumulation of Eurodollars abroad, money we borrowed so we could consume and invest and support an Asian client beyond our actual production; with a Social Security system guaranteed to go bust because the actuarial principles on which it was built all assumed continually increasing birth cohorts; and in the more sophisticated and presumably forward-looking communities (especially but not exclusively New York City and New York State), with a burden of municipal debt that territorially restricted jurisdictions cannot possibly support.

As our ancestors liked to say, it's an ill wind that blows nobody any good. Because of the birthrates in the 1950s, the back half of the 1970s will see new household formations at a rate of 2 million or so every year, guaranteeing a strong demand for new housing, new appliances, furniture, even automobiles. In the absence of folly, this basic demand for consumer durables will guarantee the prosperity of the latter 1970s, pulling us through Arab blackmail and the unwisdom of the Clean Air Act without unbearable damage. But we must use this breathing space intelligently, for the sharply declining birthrates of the years since 1965 (we were below 3.2 million births in 1973 and 1974, down from 4.3 million in the peak years of the late 1950s) mean not just smaller school populations soon, and smaller university populations in the 1990s, but reduced consumer demand and danger of truly catastrophic depression at the end of the century, when the productive work force will be the highest in our history. It is by no means too early to start stockpiling the plans and policies we will need in a quarter of a century.

6

In general, the message of this book is that Occam lives: the more fundamental the explanation, the more likely its validity, and its utility in the process of deciding what to do next. Reductionist logic is out of fashion these days, but it is still the best way to get a grip on the world, and on yourself. From this position, asking your indulgence for certain unspoken (and unoriginal) assumptions about the human condition in general, I now propose to examine some of the events and "issues" of the recent past and immediate future, to see how much that makes them surprising can be explained or simplified by reference to these four forces. I know that people do not always behave rationally, and that any analysis resting on the assumption that they do can go dangerously wrong. (Awarding an honorary degree to the entomologist William Morton Wheeler in 1930, A. Lawrence Lowell of Harvard cited him as "profound student of the social life of insects, who has shown that they also can maintain complex communities without the use of reason.") But most of the time we will be better off if we do behave rationally; and in a number of the situations discussed in these pages we simply must. The fact that we must does not mean that we can (proofs are easier than existence theorems); still, it seems worth trying.

Let us begin by considering demographic waves and related changes in the composition of the work force and the organization of social institutions—because demographic changes are central to any intelligent analysis, because the facts are beyond dispute, and because they do explain some very familiar phenomena rarely examined in this focus.

3

Age, Sex, and Employment

It would be very surprising if variations in the basic conditions of reproduction, livelihood and survival chances, that is, in the supply of and demand for human beings, with all it implies in the spacing of people, the size of markets, the role of children, the society's feeling of vitality or senescence, and many other intangibles, failed to influence character.

—David Riesman, Nathan Glazer, and Reuel Denney, The Lonely Crowd

1

Before the late 1940s, the number of live births in the United States was one of our most stable statistics, year after year. In twenty-one of the thirty-seven years from 1909 through 1945, that number was between 2.75 and 3 million. During the depression decade 1931–40, which produced the entrants to maturity of the years soon after World War II, the number of live births ranged from 2.3 million to 2.56 million. Then, in 1946, there were 3.4 million births; the next year the number jumped farther, to 3.8 million, and in 1953 it crossed the 4 million mark.

School enrollment, which had risen only from 23 million in 1920 to 28 million in 1950, jumped to 36 million in 1956 and 44 million in 1962. Eventually, inexorably, these huge age cohorts moved into the job market. At the peak period of World War II arms production, when old men were being called from chimney corners to drive fork-lift trucks and Rosie was on the night shift riveting, employment in America topped out at 54 million; and at war's end Henry Wallace made himself the McGovern of his day by calling for an impossible target of 60 million jobs. In early 1975, an American economy that was supplying 84 million jobs (one million *more* than two years before) saw unemployment rise to a frightening level of 9 percent—and faced the need to generate 2 million new jobs every year to keep the unemployment rate from rising even higher.

These are developments of truly earthquake dimensions in social and economic history. If, as the Census Bureau had expected (the difficulties of prediction, again), the upward trend of birthrates had proved a permanent phenomenon in American society, we would soon have to face exquisitely difficult decisions about the role of government in restricting production, resettling surplus populations, allocating access to health services, recreational facilities, ultimately water and probably food. But in the mid-1970s the ratio between the number of births and the number of women of child-bearing age had dropped so low that in the absence of immigration the nation would eventually begin to lose population: the birth cohorts of 1973 and 1974 were down below 3.2 million. The result, then, has been a single twenty-year bulge of very large age cohorts, moving along the snake of time as an undigestible mass that will in each period distort the functioning of the institutions of American society.

Americans born in the decade 1946–56 started life in hospital corridors, were mothered in too-small apartments or overstuffed suburban boxes, schooled on double sessions in crowded classrooms. Those who went to college were likely to be processed as mechanically as possible through facilities originally planned for perhaps half as many students; those who did not go to college often found themselves in that great waste barrel of the latter 1960s, the U.S. Army in Vietnam. Reaching the age when they could open their mouths as a group, they said, not surprisingly, that "the system" didn't work right anymore.

The extent of the crisis—indeed, despite the talk of a "population explosion," the very fact that there *was* a crisis—was masked by technology and affluence. In earlier times, so rapid a growth of population (especially nonproductive population) would have put pressure on the food supply and on sanitary facilities. "Unless an emigration takes place," Thomas Malthus wrote, "the deaths will shortly exceed the births. . . . Were there no other depopulating causes, every country would, without doubt, be subject to periodical pestilences or famines."

Instead, food production expanded so rapidly in America that diet improved (a miracle little appreciated at the time, because it was always being presented as a "farm problem"; the fact is that between 1950 and 1970 American agricultural production increased by two-thirds while employment on American farms dropped by two-thirds, and the proportion of average American family income spent on food was reduced from not quite one-quarter to not quite one-sixth). And medical technology reduced the incidence of disease so effectively that these societally very vulnerable huge age cohorts grew up with a sense of personal invulnerability never known before. Dr. Lewis Thomas puts it definitively: "Until a few decades ago . . . we moved, with our families, in and out of death. We had lobar pneumonia, meningococcal meningitis, streptococcal infections, diphtheria, endocarditis, enteric fevers, various septicemias, syphilis, and, always, everywhere, tuberculosis. Most of these have now left us, thanks to antibiotics, plumbing, civilization, and money." Dr. Thomas adds, "But we remember." He speaks for an earlier generation: the young, now young adults, have no such memories. Salk had banished polio before they could even read the newspapers.

Both business and government were sluggish in responding to the needs of the expanding American family of 1946–56. (So was academia. David Riesman had rested the argument of *The Lonely Crowd* on the end of the era of population increase; republishing a substantially edited version in paperback in 1953, he noted that "the birthrate has shown an uncertain tendency to rise again, which most demographers think is temporary.") It is, I think, significant that the first major penetration by Japanese manufactured goods in the American economy came in products for the youth market: motorcycles, transistor radios and portable phonographs, cheap guitars. But once we moved, being rich and clever, we moved far.

In the fifteen years from 1931 through 1945, we had built only 4.6 million new dwelling units—this despite Franklin Roosevelt's proclaimed determination to better the condition of the "one-third of a nation" that was "ill-housed." In the five years 1946 through 1950 we added another 4.6 million, and in the five years 1951 through 1956 we built 5.9 million. In the *two* years 1971 and 1972, when the baby-boom children began to need homes of their own, more new housing was added to the American stock than had been built in the entire fifteen-year period 1931–45.

Similarly with education: expenditures on the public schools rose from less than $3 billion in 1946 to almost $6 billion in 1950, $11 billion in 1956, crossing the $20 billion mark in 1963. By 1972, educators were claiming that the schools were starved though their budgets were over $50 billion a year. And inflation accounts for only a relatively small part of these increases—in 1946 we were spending 1.5 percent of the gross national product on public schools, but by 1972 we were spending 4.7 percent.

The young born in the second half of the twenty-year bulge, then, were much better served by society than their older brothers and sisters; and they are, again not surprisingly (though the newspapers are surprised), much less nuisance to manage, much less disenchanted with "the system." But there are still too many of them; and they must expect trouble down the road.

2

The baby boom was also, unavoidably, a mother boom. Though the figures are not kept this way, it seems that at any time during the 1950s *most* American women between the ages of twenty and thirty were either pregnant or caring for one or more children under the age of five.

Betty Friedan has described at length the social pressures to which American (and European) women were subjected in the years immediately after the war. In the 1930s, marriage rates in America had only once, in 1937, risen as high as 75 per 1,000 unmarried women; from 1941 through 1950, this rate averaged 92.3. In 1920, the proportion of never-married American females over the age of fourteen was 24.1; in 1940, it was 24.3; in 1960, it was 18.4. Women whose psychosexual needs would have permitted them to remain single in previous generations were married in the years around 1950, and produced children. Of every thousand women who turned twenty-three in 1940, 386 had produced at least one child; of every thousand who turned twenty-three in 1955, 583 had given birth. Without anyone's planning it that way, a large fraction of American womanhood was withdrawn from the labor market by the need to provide services to the young outside the market economy. But these age cohorts moved on to stages where they consumed more goods and services that had to be provided outside the home—and in the affluence of the 1960s they consumed more per capita than any previous generation, multiplying the already considerable burden of their numbers. The work force had to expand if this economic demand was to be met.

Some of the need for new labor was satisfied as it always had been in American history: by the release of agricultural labor to the city through the intermediation of improved farm technology. Much of this labor was southern Negro, and the demand for workers by industrial society fueled the civil rights movement of the late 1950s and early 1960s. But as the birthrate went down, as the children grew up, as the jobs moved increasingly out to the suburbs to be near the work force, women began entering the labor market in unprecedented numbers. Between 1960 and 1970, the number of women working in America rose from 20 million to 30 million, and the proportion of women in the work force rose from barely a third to almost two-fifths. In 1972, about 44 percent of all American women over the age of sixteen were working, as against about 76 percent of the men.

In historical focus, of course, all such statistics are cultural artifacts. There is a much smaller proportion of the female population "working" today than was working in the early years of the republic, when 80-odd percent of the population lived on farms; the farmer's wife was an integral part of the work force, as important as the horse. "Cottage industries" in the years before the industrial revolution had been to a great extent female in their work force, and women were put to work from the beginning in the power-driven factories: in 1831, four-fifths of the workers in Massachusetts textile mills were women. The reduction in the proportion of women gainfully employed in the latter nineteenth and the twentieth centuries reflected the horrifyingly burdensome physical conditions of factory work at the time (which led women to withdraw from the labor force if they could, and persuaded legislatures to write laws that made the employment of women less profitable to entrepreneurs) and also the fact that married women were kept almost continually pregnant, which diminished their reliability in a narrowly structured production process.

Social roles are sex related in every culture, and the elements that determine these roles lie deep in each national soul. In the Soviet Union, the great majority of dentists and of street cleaners are women, while in America the sight of a woman in either of these capacities still provokes reactions not unlike those provoked in Sam Johnson by a lady preacher. Gradually, everywhere, technology changes perceptions of "women's work." The typewriter facilitates the replacement of the clerk by the secretary; power steering makes lady cabbies and even truck drivers.

Thanks to machinery, air conditioning, and noise control, work has become much less nasty—only in the civil services, the police and fire departments, and the imagination of sociologists has work become more degrading and unpleasant in recent years. Machines may or may not dehumanize (in itself, perhaps not a bad thing); they certainly de-fatigue. Meanwhile, the technology of "labor-saving devices," the washing machines and frozen foods and self-cleansing ovens, enables women to do the world's work and their own work, and still keep their looks. And here the market mechanism responded quickly to need, producing not only the home machinery but also the "convenience food" industry, the rash of Kentucky Fried Chickens, McDonaldses and the like, that serves the needs of the two-worker family.

Taken at ten-year intervals, the figures in the United States show a fairly steady growth in the female proportion of the labor force, tending to rise more rapidly in more recent years—from 20 percent in 1920 to 22 percent in 1930, 24 percent in 1940, 29 percent in 1950, 33 percent in 1960, 38 percent in 1970. But the fluctuations within the decades—and within the age cohorts of females—have been considerable. The peak participation rate for women during World War II was not exceeded until the 1960s; and it was 1970 before participation by women aged twenty to twenty-four regained the levels achieved in 1944. Most of the growth in the female work force has been among older women—starting in the mid-1950s, for the first time since such figures have been gathered, the proportion of women aged forty-five to sixty-four who are in the labor market has been greater than the proportion of women twenty-five to forty-four.

More importantly, the extraordinary pressure to procreate in the 1950s had worked a change in the nature of and attitudes toward female employment. Husbands and children had absorbed the energies that in the generations just before would have gone into self-promotion, feminist or otherwise. Quantitatively, the proportion of women in the job market had dropped only a few percentage points and would soon begin to rise again; qualitatively, the decline was more serious.

Women tend to wind up with poorly paid jobs (this is the deceptive link between the women's movement and the Negro movement); they like the sociability of the office bullpen, say the insurance companies; they are good at tiny-work, says the proprietor of the electronics assembly line. Still, occupational choice is one of those areas where an individual of genius—an Elizabeth Blackwell, an Eve Curie, a Jane Addams—can literally break a path that others will follow. It is often a narrow path —if a woman wins a Nobel prize in chemistry for work with crystals, subsequent generations of female chemistry students will be told to take up crystallography because "it's a woman's field"—but it's a path.

Paths go somewhere, however, only if people choose to take them. In the 1950s, the biological imperatives that were producing the astonishing birthrate were also dissuading young women from competing against men for leadership roles. Even in fields where women had historically held executive positions men increasingly took over the best jobs—before the war, more than half the nation's elementary schools had female principals; by the 1960s, only a quarter of these jobs were held by women. The proportion of doctorates and other graduate degrees earned by women in 1970 was still below that of the women of 1930.

At each educational level, the average annual income of women declined through the postwar years by relation to the average annual income of men. In 1950, women with four years of college earned about 53 percent as much as men with four years of college; by 1970, their earnings were only 44 percent as great as those of men with equivalent certifications. The howl of rage in the women's movement can be explained more satisfactorily by the study of such statistics than by the puzzling out of the fustian in the magazines and the books of feminist poetry.

The recruitment of women back into the labor market began because a society with increasing numbers in its nonproductive age cohorts (the burgeoning young and the surviving aged) needed more helping hands. By the late 1960s, with the postwar baby crop entering the job market, women were no longer needed in such numbers—but, insistently, as never before in history, they remained at work.

The felt needs of the working-class but middle-income family could be met only by two incomes—positively, in terms of the clothes and color TVs and second homes and vacation trips the woman's job can buy; negatively, in terms of such goodies already bought and being paid off on the installment plan. Two decades ago, Barbara Ward wrote of "the revolution of rising expectations" that created social strain in the underdeveloped lands that had learned about living conditions in the West. By one of the great ironies of history, that revolution struck not in the impoverished countries (which were too far behind even to hope to reach European standards within the time horizons of political leadership) but in the developed world itself.

The strength of the women's movement (which must be distinguished from the howl) derives, like the strength of other mass movements, from its participants' objectively perceived insecurities. Quite a lot of women's jobs are marginal: the female work force is first to be fired not only because it was last to be hired but also because it is the most dispensable. Like the Jewish Defense League, the women's movement says, Never Again. This time around, at whatever price, the women intend to keep their jobs.

The age cohorts of the baby boom come to maturity, then, in a job market that must absorb an unprecedented proportion of their women as well as their men—and must also expand the job opportunities offered to older women. The victims, for reasons we shall examine *infra*, are going to be the lower two-thirds of the Negro community. It would be nice if one could talk dispassionately about this problem. I do not quarrel with the proposition that more and better jobs (obviously including leadership jobs) must be opened on a more equitable basis to skilled and trained women who can contribute the result of that skill and training to the common enterprise. And in the next century, despite all the machinery we will have, I fancy we will want in the labor force all the women we can get, skilled or otherwise. But not now. Quite apart from the 1974–76 recession, this is an awful time to encourage young mothers and older married women to take and hold the unskilled and entry-level jobs that might otherwise be available to adolescents.

3

The most significant influence exerted on society by the existence of these extraordinary age cohorts was the crime wave, for among the characteristics of the young is that they get in trouble with the law. The Children's Bureau has estimated that between the ages of ten and seventeen as much as a fifth of all boys will make some contact with a juvenile court. Three-fifths of all serious crime in America is committed by adolescents and young men between the ages of fifteen and twenty-four—a group that grew by 50 percent between 1960 and 1970.

It seems fair to say that we handled this situation badly. At precisely the time when it was most important to convince the young that criminal activity would be a losing proposition, our criminologists abandoned this goal entirely and went chasing after the butterfly of rehabilitation; the leading textbook in criminology haughtily dismissed the idea of deterrence as "simply a derived rationalization of revenge." Meanwhile, our appellate courts wholeheartedly adopted the philosophy Roscoe Pound once described as "the sporting theory of justice." ("The inquiry is not," he said, "What do substantive law and justice require? Instead, the inquiry is: Have the rules of the game been carried out strictly? If any material infraction is discovered, just as the football rules put back the offending team five or ten or fifteen yards, as the case may be, our sporting theory of justice awards new trials, or reverses judgments. . . ." These words were spoken in 1906.)

Nothing could be more damaging to the socialization of the

young than this transference from the question of whether or not they did something wrong (a question even the most poorly brought up had to confront occasionally at home *and among friends*) to the question of whether those accusing them had followed every byway of approved procedure. The social effect of reforms in the juvenile court system and criminal procedure was to convince a huge generation of the truth of Sam Weller's observation that the law is a ass. Lost entirely was the sense that, in the words of law professor Francis Allen, "the criminal law has a general preventive function . . . that the influence of criminal sanctions on the millions who never engage in serious criminality is of greater social importance than their impact on the hundreds of thousands who do."

I watched this process play itself out from a peculiar vantage point, on a New York City local school board with responsibilities extending into one of the worst crime districts in the city. Deprived of support from the criminal justice system—or from the great organs of opinion, which through the 1960s looked rather indulgently on black crime—the home, the school, and the church all lost ground to the street. It is no more than guesswork to say that a concerted attack on the dominance of the street, harrying the gangs and systematically humiliating their leaders, would have prevented the present situation in the urban slums, where "terror survives the ruin it has gorged." The breakup of families in a transplanted rural community stunned by the anonymity of the cities might well have blunted the most calculated intervention by the most tough-minded government. I cannot believe, though, that we would be worse off than we are.

Spilt milk: the street has won, and not until the mid-1980s will diminishing age cohorts give us a chance to do more than make foundations for the rebuilding of urban institutions. Long after today's urban young have grown up and moved to the suburbs, blighted areas of our central cities will testify to the harm done by the simultaneous expansion of the numbers of young men and the extent of their "rights."

Less important than the growth of crime but more visible as a function of the baby boom (because crime has not been seen as a "youth problem") was the exaggeration of the youth cult never entirely absent from America. For the adult members of the immigrant family, it had always been a kind of death to leave familiar byways and language and come to the new world; the justification was the opportunity for their children. Writing at the high point of immigration to America, John Dewey looked ahead to a "century of the child." It came fifty years later.

James Coleman and his colleagues of the Panel on Youth of the President's Science Advisory Committee distinguished three historical periods in American attitudes toward the young —the time when they were needed to contribute to the family income (on the farm or in the factory); the time when the family could afford to dispense with their income and sent them to school; and finally the time when they were awarded the right to a share of the discretionary income of the household. In the accelerating affluence of the 1960s, the young acquired increasing purchasing power. They used it to buy psychic space that would be all their own: what those who pandered to them, for commercial or personal reasons, called a counterculture.

Through the 1950s and 1960s, our huge age cohorts grew up in a state of virtual isolation from the productive economic life of the society. Very few had more than the most remote idea of what their fathers (and mothers) did outside the home; it had long been exceptional rather than normal in America for a son to plan to follow his father's occupation. The idea of rising to an occupation through apprenticeship had been discarded both inside and outside the home: extended schooling was to substitute for the training previous generations had gained through experience. Thus young people were deprived not only of the historically established occupational support supplied by their families, but also of the emotional support while growing into a career that had once been supplied by the stable personal relations of master and apprentice.

Such concerns were submerged, quite out of sight, until very recently, because American society had made an almost conscious decision to keep the young at school and college as long as they could possibly be held there. The reasons why are complicated and varied. Americans have long believed in education as a thing in itself and in longer years of schooling as an independent value; John Dewey insisted that "advance in civilization is an accompaniment of the prolongation of infancy." And as the baby boom neared the age of employment, the labor unions were insistent on the need to keep young people out of the job market as long as possible. Seniority provisions were strengthened in all union contracts to guarantee that the young of the 1970s could not, like the young of all previous periods, make a place for themselves by competing against the older generation. I would argue that subconsciously the young of the 1960s recognized this sea change in their prospects, and that the slogan "never trust anybody over thirty" expressed a legitimate if unanalyzed bitterness.

Pressure for increases in the minimum wage was brought on the legislatures partly for their indirect benefit to union members (all of whom were working for scales above the minimum wage but stood to benefit from a general upward push), mostly to strengthen the protection of the existing work force against what is inevitably cut-rate competition. A high minimum wage held down youth employment because the average adolescent —lacking work habits and work savvy, prone to change jobs frequently—was not worth what the government said he had to be paid. In the absence of a pull from the job market, there was little reason not to stay in school (when the economy overinflated in 1972, first-time college enrollment dipped substantially; in the mounting recession of fall 1974, first-time enrollment rose). And until the end of the draft, of course, college was much favored as the most desirable way to postpone, and perhaps avoid, military service and the threat of Vietnam.

But the prime reason why so many young people continued to college was the incessantly reiterated and advertised promise that a college education was the best, even the only, route to a white-collar future and a good income. For some years the American Council on Education has conducted a large-scale survey of the attitudes of incoming freshmen at the nation's colleges and universities. In the version of this opinion poll employed in 1971, ACE asked the new arrivals why they were going to college, and by an overwhelming margin (especially among the males) the first answer was "to get a better job." The question was not asked again in later years, presumably because the response was considered unsatisfactory.

The effort to keep youngsters in school was remarkably successful. James Coleman reports that "while the population of 16- to 19-year-olds increased between 1957 and 1970 by 6 million, the 'not enrolled in school' labor force component of this age group increased by only 0.6 million. Similarly, in the 20–24 age group, which increased by 6.5 million between 1960 and 1970, the 'not enrolled' labor force increased by only 2 million in the same period." But every year since 1970, the problem has become less manageable by this tactic, partly because the young do get older and dribble out of even the most extended educational program, partly because the brute numbers are still increasing. The first 4-million age cohort turned twenty in 1973, and from then till 1984 we shall have to absorb every year *80 percent more* twenty-year-olds than we had to absorb in any year of the 1950s. We have not given much thought to what we want them to do. The strongest criticism of American higher education, said Reck Niebuhr of Temple in 1969, is that "it fails to *conceptualize* its manpower function."

And the one large section of the educational enterprise that did give specific career direction was disastrously wrong. The first purpose of American higher education had always been teacher training, and to the extent that secondary education was a preparation for college the "future teacher" component had always been important in high school, too. In the 1950s and 1960s, education was the most rapidly expanding growth industry in the country, and its leaders quite naturally prepared for continuing increases in employment. The momentum of this drive was such that the number of teachers continued to rise after the falling birthrate had started to reduce the number of pupils in the schools.

Over the period 1962–63 to 1972–73, the average daily register at public elementary and secondary schools rose only 17.2 percent, from 38.6 million to 45.2 million, while the total instructional staff in the schools rose 42.3 percent, from 1.65 million to 2.35 million. Into the 1970s, the colleges of education simply ignored the declining birthrate, and continued to train larger and larger numbers of students for careers as teachers. The bubble burst with the class of 1973: in spring 1974, no fewer than 128,000 young teachers who had been licensed the previous June had still not been able to find jobs in schools. Another 110,000 joined their ranks in June 1974.

On the college teaching level, the discrepancy between expectable demand and planned supply was even more dramatic —and even less excusable, for Allan Cartter of the American Council on Education had publicly demonstrated as early as 1965 that by the 1980s the need for new PhDs to teach in colleges would drop to zero. (In fact, it will drop below zero: on Cartter's 1972 projections, which by 1974 looked optimistic, the colleges would have too many professors in 1985–88 even if they hired nobody at all in those years.) Nevertheless, the output of new PhDs rose from less than ten thousand a year in 1960 to more than thirty-four thousand in 1972. A reasonable guess at mid-decade is that half of the graduate students who hope to use their PhD as an entry to teaching on the college level will find themselves disappointed—and the proportion of the unlucky will rise in the 1980s.

The education community has continued to be astonishingly resistant to the implications of the declining birthrate. In 1974 the Educational Facilities Laboratory of the Ford Foundation published a pamphlet dealing with surplus space in school systems and the uses to which it could be put. One section of the pamphlet dealt with enrollment projections. "We can be quite sure of the size of the enrollment decline through 1980," the pamphlet announced, and gave the figure as 2.3 million below 1973 totals—though the population of school age will go down about 6 million between 1973 and 1980. EFL's graph that projects high school enrollments shows a top of 15.9 million in 1975 and a bottom of 14.0 million in 1985, with the numbers turning up thereafter (and on one of the three alternative projections passing the 1975 peak by 1988). But all the students who will be in high school in 1987 (and three-quarters of those who will be in high school in 1988) were already born before the EFL pamphlet went to press; it was "quite sure" that the declining trend in enrollment would last until at least 1988, and that the bottom would be hit at 12 million, if the decline stopped there. This is not opinion, to be argued about; it is information.

Elephantiasis was everywhere in American higher education in the early 1970s. By the middle of the decade, the law schools were turning out new lawyers at a rate of twenty-five thousand a year, up from less than ten thousand a year in the 1950s—even though the spread of no-fault insurance promised to take away from the legal profession that quarter of its income traditionally derived from automobile accident cases. But the real tragedy lies on the undergraduate college level, where millions of young Americans have been drawn by hopes that cannot be realized—and other millions will suffer for it.

Since the latter 1960s, roughly half of each age cohort has gone to college, up from roughly one quarter in the mid-1950s. By the most charitable estimates of the Labor Department, however, only 13 to 14 percent of the new jobs that will be available in the fourth quarter of the century will be jobs of the kind that traditionally required a college education, which means that half the college graduates (not to mention all the dropouts) will find less reward for their efforts than they had been led to anticipate.

Worries that American colleges would produce an overeducated unemployed intellectual proletariat have been commonplace since Seymour Harris of Harvard first uttered them in

1947; but it hasn't happened, and it won't. What does happen in the American cultural context is something worse: jobs that were once available without educational credentials are redefined to require them, to assure college graduates (by definition, the children of the middle class) a protected market of sufficient size. The price is therefore paid by those who do not go to college (predominantly the children of the working class), whose opportunities are artificially and quite unnecessarily restricted. The headlong rush to a credentialed society was checked to a degree by the civil rights movement, representing mostly a Negro community of lesser educational attainments; and in the Duke Power case in 1971, the Supreme Court held that educational criteria could not be used in determining eligibility for employment in the absence of some reasonable demonstration that the education was required by the job. In a pinch, however, such demonstrations can be supplied for enough jobs to insure the continued growth of credentialism— and the colleges, faced with the prospect of diminished enrollment from the smaller age cohorts of the future, must intensify both their overt and their subtle efforts to convince government licensing bodies, large employers, and the young that a college education is a necessity.

Arriving at maturity, then, the members of the huge age cohorts confront an economy where there are not enough jobs to go round, and nowhere near enough of the kinds of jobs considered proper for a liberally educated man to absorb the supply of newcomers certified as liberally educated. The solution for the educated will be the preemption of a higher proportion of the available jobs for their exclusive occupancy, and there will be no solution for large numbers of those who started off unlucky in nature or nurture.

Significantly, the first person to single out this danger was the black psychologist Kenneth Clark. "The major problem which confronts contemporary youth," he wrote in 1957, "is not that they will be prematurely exploited by an industrial economy that is insatiable in its demand for manpower, but that they will .

be excluded from that participation in the economy that is essential for the assumption of independent economic and adult status. The vestibule stage of adolescence may be prolonged to a point where social and psychological stresses on young people may present for them and the society a most severe problem. . . . A second and related threat to young people may be the abstract threat of a sense of exclusion."

Obviously, some kinds of work are more rewarding than others; but any work at all is better than none. The real horror of aging, as old people are always saying, is the feeling that "I'm no use to anybody anymore." The old men in the village squares in France, the bewildered peasants in the shanty towns around the cancerous cities of the tropics, the miserable kids on Telegraph Road in Berkeley and the dropouts on the stoops of the South Bronx—all are living testimony to the emptiness of purposeless existence. Work, as Freud pointed out sixty years ago, is man's *positive* relation to society, his reason for believing that his neighbors are better off because he lives, and thus essential to even the most minimally positive self-image. The despairing sense that there will *never* be jobs for them is not unrelated to the identification with the street and the acceptance of criminality as a norm by black adolescents.

4

A surplus of labor from a high birthrate and the eviction of the peasantry from the farms created in Britain the long, gradual deflation of the second half of the nineteenth century. This peaceful, profitless prosperity produced the modern world in more ways than one, because its observation stimulated in Karl Marx his peculiar vision of the future of capitalism. Competition for jobs drove down money wages (neither depressing nor raising the low standard of living, because the gradually reduced pay envelope continued to buy about as much as before). Meanwhile, the price of interest-bearing assets tended to rise, reducing the apparent "profit" on capital, because the value of a given quantity of earnings was ever-increasing. Marx saw an inevitable squeeze on the working classes coupled with an "iron law" of diminishing profits, until capitalism collapsed in a crisis of underconsumption. Splendidly impervious to evidence, the theory, unfortunately, survives.

The legacy of Malthus and Marx and other nineteenth-century economists has made it difficult for today's analysts of social phenomena to understand the changes that affluence and technology have wrought in the pressures that unusually large age cohorts now apply to their community. It is taken for granted today that each new arrival must be provided with food, clothing, and shelter to a minimal quality that would have seemed luxury in the nineteenth (or early twentieth) century; and a high birthrate thus tends to increase substantially, within a few years, the quantity of national product that must be consumed here and now rather than saved for the future. Meanwhile, technology requires that each new job be backed by capital investments of a size that would have been unimaginable as recently as a generation ago. In the United States over the next decade, 2 million new jobs a year will be required simply to keep an already high unemployment rate from rising farther. In 1975 dollars, the average capital cost per job is something over $40,000. Thus an annual investment of $80 billion—more than 6 percent of the net national income—will be required simply to absorb the new workers and maintain the average real income of members of the work force. (Jobs created without the minimum capital investment presumably yield less output per man-hour worked, thus reducing the workers' average product and, unavoidably, average income.) In the absence of effective conscious or automatic procedures for long-range decision-making, the simultaneous demand for increased consumption and increased capital accumulation generates an accelerating inflation.

We shall look in the next chapter at some of the rather surprising real effects of inflation on a highly developed economy dominated by the quest for affluence and by technological change. In the conflict of interest among generations, however, it seems clear enough that inflation benefits the young at the expense of their elders. Much of the wealth of the community is held in the form of titles to money—savings accounts, government bonds, insurance policies. Inflation depreciates the real value of these titles to money, few of which are owned by the young. Though alert entrepreneurs and speculators can make a good thing of inflation, most already established citizens are losers. Greater shares of the national product will go to current earnings rather than to stored wealth—and the young can fight with some success for their just proportion of current earnings. The provision of consumer credit allows the young to accumulate what the economist Harry Johnson has called "consumer capital"—the automobile, the appliances in the kitchen and the laundry room, even the house itself—at bargain prices, because the loan taken when the purchase is made can be paid off from ever-rising salaries in money of ever-depreciating value. Interest rates rise, but not that much (especially on consumer loans, which are politically sensitive). The fact that inflation benefits the debtor class at the cost of the creditor class means that it benefits the young at the expense of their parents. Thus very large young cohorts produce continuing political pressure for inflationary policies.

Unfortunately, an inflation-prone society is, as we shall see, an uncomfortable environment in which to live. As they achieve full maturity, today's young will find themselves deprived of that satisfying sense of accomplishment and security which has historically made early middle age "the prime of life." Indeed, about the only time one can honestly predict happiness for most of the children we brought into the world in such numbers in the 1950s is their later middle age, when their own children are no longer a burden, the housing and capital accumulations of the past will be entirely adequate, high personal consumption will become socially desirable, and it will be truly practical to clean up the environment because the capital investment funds required for this purpose will no longer be needed for the creation of jobs. The time for "no growth" will come when there is no growth.

Our story of the bulge in the demographic snake has, however, a horrible ending. No generation goes out happily: "second childishness," Jaques said, "and mere oblivion—/ Sans teeth, sans eyes, sans taste, sans everything." Now there will be more of that than ever before. By all indications, the generation now reaching maturity will be the first in history to be denied as a group nature's blessing of a death that relates to the end of the possibilities of a meaningful life. This is a peculiarly painful subject, and about the only author who has been willing to face it head on is Marion Levy of Princeton. "One of the most radical changes" in modern life, he writes, is that "we take it for granted that practically everyone will survive into senility." Elsewhere, Levy has written sardonically that when the Chinese achieve the full benefits of modern technology "we shall see a day in which if senile Chinese are wheeled four abreast past a given point, their procession will never end. . . . Many if not most of the glories of filial piety rest on the fact that very few of the younger generation have had to cope with the senility of the older generation. With modernization all of us will have to find a way."

By 1975, more than a tenth of the American population was over sixty-five years old, as against only 4 percent in 1900. (The rapid growth of the over-sixty-five proportion of the population, incidentally, is the most important reason why the popular analysis of income distribution that breaks the nation into five equal classes shows the bottom 20 percent with no increase in income share. It is a real if inadequate accomplishment of American society, not a condemnation, that the share of the bottom fifth in the general prosperity has remained constant though a rapidly increasing proportion of that bottom fifth, old people and Negro families headed by females, is unproductive and has no economic source of income.) In what may turn out to be the most dramatically unfair action against the outsize age cohorts of the twenty-year bulge, their parents in 1971 rewrote the social security laws to assure themselves a highly comfortable retirement at four to five times the monthly income social security yields today—based not on the social security taxes they were paying themselves but on the taxes that will be paid by the larger work force coming on. But when the demographic bulge reaches retirement age, *their* successors will be too few to support so many old people in so fine a style: the unfunded liabilities of the social security system will then total well over $2 *trillion* of today's dollars. Assuming only a minor growth in longevity from all the medical research now in progress, a social security tax rate approaching 30 percent of the national payroll will then be necessary to meet the payouts prescribed by law, and nobody believes that social security taxes of those dimensions will actually be assessed.

The work of reneging on the promises has already begun. Early in 1975, the Social Security Advisory Council recommended to Congress changes in the benefit provisions of the law that would not take effect until after the year 2000. Their effect would be to reduce by about 30 percent the benefits that those retiring after that year would have received without the change in the law, and to postpone the permissible age of retirement with full entitlements. By 2011, when the children born immediately after World War II reach sixty-five, the age of retirement would reach sixty-six; by 2018, when the first over 4-million age cohort reaches sixty-five, the age of retirement would rise to sixty-seven; by 2024, when the tip-top peak age cohort of 1959 will be sixty-five, the age of retirement would be set at sixty-eight. Informed that these changes were being recommended, the congressmen most closely involved with social security legislation reacted with outrage—and no doubt the law will not be changed for some years. But some change of that sort will almost certainly come, because the only alternative is an immediate substantial increase in today's social security taxes, and nobody is going to vote for that—not today's middle-aged, who would get nothing from it, and not today's young, whose time horizons rise nowhere near high enough to encompass their own retirement.

I say "almost certainly," because this unfortunate generation does have one advantage that will persist: in a democratic society, big age cohorts have big voting strength. More than any ethnic group, the aged can be welded into a united political force, and an elderly community much smaller than the retirement cadre of the early twenty-first century is already beginning to demonstrate remarkable clout in defining political issues for their own benefit. Some of the strength of the senior citizen lobbies derives from the guilt the middle-aged feel (and should feel) about their neglect of their aging parents, their willingness to slough off onto society as a whole what were once regarded as the most sacrosanct of human responsibilities. But that is what Marion Levy was talking about when he warned of the difficulties of adjusting to a future characterized by mass senility. At best, it is going to be very messy.

Of course, we are not likely to get so severe a relative overload of old people as a straight-line projection of the birth cohorts of the last few years would predict. Birthrates are still cyclical; and more than half the girls born in our baby boom have not yet reached the age of reproduction. For the number of live births in the United States to remain at the 1974 figure of 3.2 million a year would require in the 1980s a birthrate of about 80 a year for each 1,000 women between the ages of eighteen and thirty-eight, which would be only half the rate in their parents' generation and 30 percent below even today's historic lows. Still, it does seem unlikely that America will ever again in a foreseeable future produce age cohorts the size of those born in the period 1946–66. Reflecting both selfish and altruistic motives, the conservation ethic will grow stronger in the years ahead; contraception will be increasingly easy and foolproof; and the battle to maintain a horror of abortion as part of our morality has already been definitively lost.

We are now at midpoint in an age that for demographic reasons alone will be unique in American history. Though it is fashionable to be very gloomy about the country's future, there will be many reasons to be glad when this present becomes the past.

4

Inflation and Priorities . . .

It was during the Inflation that the Germans forgot how to rely on themselves as individuals and learned to expect everything from "politics," from "the state," from "destiny." . . . Inflation is a tragedy that makes a whole people cynical, hardhearted and indifferent. Having been robbed, the Germans became a nation of robbers.

—Thomas Mann, 1942

1

Concern about the terms of trade between things and men, goods and services, is by no means original to our time: two centuries before J. K. Galbraith wrote bitterly about the lack of social services in an affluent society, Thomas Gray had lamented an England "where wealth accumulates and men decay." (In the Great Depression, Chesterton parodied Gray's poem: "And irony that glares like judgment day/Sees men accumulate and wealth decay.") In real life as distinguished from literature, there is no escaping the division of labor and the quest for efficiency. And with the division of labor—*pari passu,* as the economists say, in equal steps—there comes the institution of money, the commodity that can be exchanged for all other commodities and can be produced by the state. We think of ourselves as living in the nuclear age or the computer age or the age of anxiety; but history may well record that we lived in the age of credit money.

The willingness to work for money is a proof of social cohesion, the essential foundation of what Rousseau called the social contract. In Latin, "credit" means "he believes," and indeed he does. For men in modern society, money income expresses most of the sum of hope and expectation for themselves and their families both in the immediate future (the money will buy the food they eat) and over the longer term. Perhaps the most extraordinary of the misjudgments of Karl Marx and his followers was the idea that the shift to the mediation of money from the direct consumption of the fruits of labor meant man's "alienation" from his work. In truth, this profound social change means man's integration into an interdependent humanity. Reference has been made to the promotion of selfishness by two of the large technological innovations of this century, the automobile and television. Credit money, oddly enough (to speak the truth is more important than to be believed), greatly diminishes tribal selfishness, or at least its expression.

It is in societies that operate virtually without the exchange of money that one finds the deepest suspicions even of friend and neighbor, the greatest isolation of the family unit. Edward Banfield repeats a story told him by a local doctor in southern Italy: "A peasant father . . . throws his hat upon the ground. 'What did I do?' he asks one of his sons. 'You threw your hat upon the ground,' the son answers, whereupon the father strikes him. He picks up his hat and asks another son, 'What did I do?' 'You picked up your hat,' the son replies and gets a blow in his turn. 'What did I do?' the father asks the third son. 'I don't know,' the smart one replies. 'Remember, sons,' the father concludes, 'if someone asks you how many goats your father has, the answer is, you don't know.' "

Money makes possible a great increase in the number of people who feel themselves secure, and in the degree of that security. Before the universal adoption of credit money, the farmer knew himself at the mercy of forces greater than his efforts: drought or frost could blight his crops, lightning could strike the barn, kill the animals, burn the accumulated grain.

The merchant lived in continual anxiety, for the ship carrying his goods or gold could sink, the wagons could be waylaid by highwaymen. Even the courtier knew that his sovereign's tastes could change, or accident or disease could remove at a stroke all his reasons for confidence. But the nineteenth-century bourgeois accumulating consols could indeed feel that he had nothing to fear except his personalized God. And even then, not much: Dickens's Mr. Podsnap found it "very comfortable . . . that what Providence meant was invariably what Mr. Podsnap meant."

The central accomplishment of economic development in the United States over the last 150 years was not the consumer luxuries, not the relief from toil through the tapping of energy sources, not even (the best alternate candidate) the near-conquest of boredom through the miracles of telecommunication, cinema, and cheap printing. It was the possibility of relative, almost Podsnappian security for *most* Americans through stretches of life so long that security rather than danger came to seem the natural condition. The seal of certainty was placed on this creation by the welfare state, designed and organized to give those who could not achieve security by themselves a floor below which their insecurities could not fall.

As noted in the first chapter, this secular religion is a lie—the divines who called upon men to live as though each hour were their last knew more of truth than the modern savants who see salvation through health insurance—but all religions are lies in one way or another; and this one, I think, has produced a greater totality of human happiness, hour by hour on the short time horizons people actually employ, than any other faith man has ever known. For most people most of the time, its magic works: the dark goes away when you flick the switch, the doctor cures what ails you (or your baby), your wages go up and your business gets bigger, the payments amortize the mortgage on the house. Forced too far, however, security will bind and then kill the goose that lays it; and as a religion it has a painful

weakness: past a certain age, it doesn't work. (Recently, a growing realization of the cruelty of a faith that abandons man at the
end has given some of our more sensitive observers an obsession
with aging and with death as a process rather than as an event.
The nursing home, a warehouse for the dying, proves to be—
unsurprisingly—a less than satisfactory solution. This concern is
the reverse of Marion Levy's coin: the honor accorded to the
few who survived human insecurity and lived to a great age
becomes impatience at the many who cherished their safety
and lingered.) Nevertheless, security for self and family remains
the grail sought by the majority of adults in a developed
economy. Inflation destroys the hope of achieving it.

Historically, a little inflation has not necessarily been harmful
to society. "The tendency of money to depreciate," Keynes
wrote in 1923, "has been in past times a weighty counterpoise
against the cumulative results of compound interest and the
inheritance of fortunes. It has been a loosening influence
against the rigid distribution of old-won wealth and the separa-
tion of ownership from activity. By this means each generation
can disinherit in part its predecessors' heirs." A little inflation,
as noted in the last chapter, benefits the young.

More recently, however, the tendency to inflation has
sharpened in all democratic societies: we have been getting a
lot of it. Charles Kindleberger breezily states the process: "If
various sectors in an economy insist on distributive shares
which add to 105 per cent of national income, and each sector
has power over the prices of goods or factors, the economy is
destined to have 5 per cent inflation a year, a deficit in its
balance-of-payments equal to 5 per cent of its national income,
or some combination of the two. When the several sectors understand what is going on, realize that nominal money increases
in prices and wages are likely to be eaten up by inflation, and
seek to anticipate price increases, the process accelerates."

Kindleberger's "sectors" may express their insistence
through either marketplace or governmental mechanisms (or
both); and my book *The Bankers* is in large part a description

of how improvements in the technology of the banking business may enable private organizations to expand the effective "money supply" at the top of a euphoric boom, even when government is trying to keep the lid on. Normally, however, the additional credit money required to fuel inflation must be created by a government, and the "cause" of inflation is the inability of governments to secure by open and aboveboard taxation the revenues that would balance their programs of expenditure.

For inflation is a tax—the only tax available to weak governments. Any sovereignty worthy of the name can enforce the credibility of its money upon those subject to its power, simply by declaring the paper to be "legal tender." (Congressman Wright Patman while chairman of the House Banking Committee liked to say that "If you offer a man dollar bills to pay what you owe him and he won't take them, you can put that money back in your pocket and declare your debt paid; that's what 'legal tender' means.") The government can thus print money to pay its bills, and that money must be accepted at the price level prevailing when the government offers it. People now have more money, but the quantity of goods and services to be bought with money has not increased; unavoidably, the price level rises. The money is worth less to each person through whose hands it passes; and a tax is thereby spread around the community and apportioned among the universe of creditors. In effect—through the intermediation of the Federal Reserve System—that is what happens when the budget of the United States government shows a large deficit.

The immediately visible social consequences can be very serious. "By a continuing process of inflation," Keynes observed in 1919, "governments can confiscate, secretly and unobserved, an important part of the wealth of their citizens. By this method they not only confiscate, but they confiscate *arbitrarily;* and, while the process impoverishes many, it actually enriches some. The sight of this arbitrary rearrangement of riches strikes not only at security, but at confidence in the equity of the existing distribution of wealth. Those to whom the system brings wind-falls beyond their deserts and even beyond their expectations or desires, become 'profiteers' who are the object of the hatred of the bourgeoisie, whom the inflation has impoverished, not less than of the proletariat. . . . The process engages all the hidden forces of economic law on the side of destruction, and does it in a manner which not one man in a million is able to diagnose."

But the destruction is even greater out of sight, in the guts of public institutions and of economic forces that developed in the half-century after Keynes wrote. Central to the character of the postwar era in the interplay of private and governmental deci-sion was the set of automatic stabilizers that smoothed the busi-ness cycle. Government expenditures being set in advance, a decline in economic activity that produced a decline in tax revenues automatically made for government deficits, which stimulated the economy. And when economic activity im-proved, the progressive income tax system assured that in-creased payments to government would eliminate or at least reduce budgetary stimuli, restraining the euphoria of the boom. The Kennedy Administration, advised by economists who thought they could work miracles, misunderstood the operation of the stabilizers and commanded the removal of what it omi-nously labeled "fiscal drag." The procedures invented in that administration to assure that the stabilizers of the system would not inhibit "growth" at the top of the cycle—the congeries of tax credits and transfer payments and mortgage subsidies—were later abused in the Johnson and Nixon administrations to promote the inflation that brought us to grief in 1974; toward the end of this book we shall examine in some detail how this disaster happened. And inflation itself then aborted the stabil-izers when economic activity turned down in 1974.

Because inflation kept pushing up the numbers, the progres-sive tax system kept increasing government receipts even at a time of economic decline. Already stretched for cash, as they always are at the top of a boom, businesses found themselves required to pay corporate profits taxes on the increased valuation of their inventories, which brought in virtually no cash (because the inventory sold at a taxable windfall profit thanks to rising prices had to be replaced at costs that were just as inflated as the prices). Consumers whose gross wages might well be rising at a rate faster than the rate of inflation found themselves with reduced purchasing power because the government took increasing proportions of their increased income. The feedback systems that had bumped the economy back up out of 1958, 1960–61, 1966 and 1969–70 no longer worked in 1974–75, placing burdens on conscious government decision-making that this process probably cannot and certainly did not intelligently carry.

Axel Leijonhufvud of UCLA argues that the multiplication of burdens on government is an inevitable consequence of inflation, regardless of previous policy, because people necessarily come to "rely relatively less on private contracts and relatively more on political compacts in trying to ensure for themselves a reliable frame for their economic lives. . . . The fact that both parties initially entered into an agreement 'voluntarily' carries much less of a guarantee that it can be carried out amicably and without rancour than is the case in a regime of stable prices." Under these circumstances, people will "use their votes and lobbies increasingly to help insure for themselves a predictable real income." But this sort of insurance is something government can only promise, not deliver.

Even worse than the disorder in Washington, however, is the process by which inflation intensifies the destructive impact of changing technology on social cohesion and on the capacity of the market system to allocate resources and inspire activities to meet the needs of the society. It is a phenomenon of the greatest importance, and though there is a great deal of discussion and agonizing about the results, the causes are not understood at all. Let us look at them.

2

For the benefit of his students at MIT, Kindleberger likes to speak of the "haircut unit" as a cross-cultural measuring tool. The argument is that in all countries where the division of labor has created a barbering class, the average price of a haircut is always roughly the same as the hourly compensation of an industrial worker. Technology has to a degree invaded barbering —there are electric clippers rather than hand clippers for the back of the neck and the sideburns—but in essence a haircut still requires almost half an hour from a trained man with a scissors. By the nature of the beast, the barber's schedule is not filled up (queue theory can be employed to prove that a supply of barbers restricted sufficiently to fill the schedule of each would produce intolerable delays for many customers); and some of what the customer pays must go to the costs of providing the barber with his shop, chair, and tools. To keep the barber's income at parity with that of the skilled worker, then, will require a price for a half-hour haircut roughly equivalent to an industrial worker's hourly wage.

But the industrial worker's output from an hour's labor is continually increasing—even in the second half of 1974, when average productivity for the nation's work force seriously declined, industrial productivity slowly improved. To make a pair of shoes takes much less of the modern worker's time in the shoe factory than it took of his grandfather's time at the shoemaker's bench. Fifty years ago, a pair of shoes sold for perhaps twelve hours' worth of an industrial worker's paycheck; today it costs perhaps five hours' worth of paycheck for comparable quality. From the point of view of the workingman, the history of the last half-century has been a long series of reductions in the price of manufactured (and agricultural) goods, looking at the price in terms of his hours worked rather than in dollars and cents. Leonard Woodcock of the United Automobile Workers supplies some numbers: in 1950, the average American needed 8.1 months of income to buy a car; in 1960, 6.2 months; in 1970,

4.7 months. That's a cheerful story, and goes far to explain why the average middle-aged industrial worker, despite relentless editorial pressure from his betters, refuses to consider himself properly "alienated."

Technology not only makes goods cheaper; it makes them better: the average factory shoe is a more satisfactory item than the average hand-made shoe of the past. Certainly the choice of lasts is much greater, which means that most people can buy shoes that fit them better than the shoes their grandfathers wore. The computer designer Robert Fano once pointed out that a carpenter with an electric drill will drill holes not just faster, but straighter. (The complaint that things don't work right anymore has been heard since the time of the Pharaohs; and the proper answer is that things have never worked right. The owner of Ford's Model T, his heart pounding from the effort of turning the starting crank, would be amazed both by the reliability of the modern automobile and by the consumerists' angst for the good old days. Among the more important facts adolescents don't learn in school is that there used to be horse manure in the streets.)

The other side of the coin, however, is that the price of services, seen in terms of hours worked, does *not* go down; indeed, it may go up. To the extent that services must be improved in quality as goods improve in quality, they almost certainly require additional inputs of working time from the people who provide them, and thus an additional price from the people who buy them. The barbering analogy proves inadequate: a good haircut today is still what it was at the turn of the century. But a good school is supposed to have only twenty-five rather than forty children in a class; and a good hospital is supposed to offer a range of services beyond the imaginings of even thirty years ago.

The basic statement of the reasons why services *must* become more costly than goods as time passes was given in 1966 by the economists William J. Baumol and William G. Bowen in their book *Performing Arts: the Economic Dilemma*. "Let us imagine an economy divided into two sectors," they wrote, "one in which productivity is rising and another in which it is constant, the first producing automobiles, and the second, performances of Haydn trios. Let us suppose that in automobile production, where technological improvements are possible, output per man-hour is increasing at an annual rate of 4 per cent, while the productivity of trio players remains unchanged year after year. Imagine now that the workers in the automobile industry recognize the changes which are taking place and persuade management to agree to a matching rise in wages. . . . Each year the average worker's wage goes up by 4 per cent, but labor output increases by exactly the same percentage. As a consequence, labor cost per unit . . . remains absolutely unchanged . . . with no rise in automotive prices necessary to maintain company profits. . . ."

Now, "suppose that the trio players somehow succeed in getting their wages raised, and that their standard of living keeps up with that of the auto workers. . . . If the earnings of string players increase by 4 per cent per year while their productivity remains unchanged, it follows that the direct labor cost per unit of their output must also rise at 4 per cent. . . . The cost per performance must have risen correspondingly. *Moreover, there is nothing in the nature of this situation to prevent the cost of performance from rising indefinitely at a compound rate.*"

The same logic applies to *all* services where output per man-hour cannot be greatly increased by technology, which means most of government and the professions, and many of the skilled trades. The barber still needs his half-hour to cut the customer's hair; the lawyer needs two hours to coach the witness to lie *sans souci;* the nurse's aide needs fifteen minutes to sponge the patient, empty the bedpan, take the temperature, and administer the aspirin; the teacher serves the same (or even a decreasing) number of students. Architecture becomes spare and unornamented, because the stonemason still needs a week to carve flowers on a capital: the Bauhaus theory of architecture was an unconscious response to the initial workings of the Baumol-Bowen dilemma. In Kindleberger's haircut unit, the price of the haircut is stable—it still costs an industrial worker's hour—but in dollars and cents it rises as rapidly as the industrial worker's wage. And we get, incidentally—especially among the young, whose income is restricted—a vogue for long hair.

The Baumol-Bowen dilemma is the real source of the developing difficulties John Kenneth Galbraith decried in *The Affluent Society*. Unfortunately, Galbraith sees the modern economic world as a conspiracy by manufacturers and advertising agencies to make people want goods which they wouldn't want if clever advertisers left their heads alone. Because economists and sociologists tend to look to the "macro" aspects of their theories, they tend not to think about what really happens day by day in the lives of real people. For the consumer, in the conditions Baumol and Bowen describe, the observable fact is that goods always look cheap by comparison with services—and under these circumstances he scarcely needs hidden persuasion to convince him to buy goods rather than services. When this resistance to paying more for services appears in the public sector—by the rejection of school budgets, for example—we call it a "tax revolt."

For the libertarian classical economist, these changes in the relative costs of goods and services are just another fact of life, to which everyone must adjust, willy-nilly. Things and services are worth no more and no less than what people will pay for them. If people don't want to buy something at a price high enough to pay the costs of providing it, the classical economist sees no reason why the state should intervene to *make* them buy it. This is a much stronger argument than casual perusal of popular political literature might lead you to believe, but it enshrines the vital weakness of economics as a discipline—its inability to develop any workable theory of demand, because its postulates require the assumption that people know what they are doing.

No doubt consumers' economic demands do represent with reasonable accuracy their personal value systems: economic value is not unrelated to deeper judgments. But those personal value systems—those beliefs about what something *should* cost

—are souvenirs of childhood and early adulthood, while the technology that determines dollars-and-cents costs is increasingly here and now. The time lag means that people always feel services are too expensive and should somehow be made cheaper—government, education, medicine, law, theater, religion, burial . . . All at one time or another are "scandals"; all (except maybe the burial) are inevitable.

Because these developments have not been understood, let alone explained, intelligent observers find themselves bitter about what seem to them social aberrations. In 1972, when the New York Public Library was in crisis, Alfred Kazin observed ironically in the *New York Times Book Review* that he felt himself fortunate to have grown up in a time of economic depression, when everyone was poor and there was enough money for libraries. But technological progress, by reducing the relative cost of goods, *dictates* that a higher proportion of a rising gross national product must be spent on services like libraries simply to keep them on an even keel. As the society becomes more prosperous, there will indeed—barring deliberate intervention by government—be "less money" (accurately, less effective purchasing power) for libraries. What is surprising —and dangerous—is that we are surprised.

The real price of anything is the "opportunity cost"—what must be given up in order to buy it. For really rich people who understand that they are really rich, the difference in price between a cloth coat and a fur coat is negligible, because nothing extra must be given up to buy the more expensive item. For a woman living on the wages of a factory worker husband, the difference between a cloth coat and a fur coat is a dishwasher, an air conditioner in the bedroom, and a second color TV. To everyone for whom money matters, values are perceived in ratio, and the sense that there is a "correct" ratio is inescapable. Technology rapidly changes the ratios of opportunity costs, while perceived values—the sense of "correctness" of relative prices—change only slowly. Even in a society where the overall price level is reasonably stable, the impact of technology on costs must distort the ratios; the purchase of a service costs progressively more in terms of goods foregone.

Let us return to the Baumol-Bowen arithmetic, assuming a 4 percent increase in the productivity of industrial workers, a zero increase in the productivity of service workers, no costs but labor costs, and a society where the total product is equally divided between goods and services. Over a period of eighteen years, the price of each unit of service (a trio concert, a course in economics, a mail delivery or an obstetrical delivery) will double, while the price of an automobile or a washing machine will remain the same.

One of our key assumptions in this example is that the total product of the economy, valued in money terms, remains equally divided between goods and services. If the two kinds of output commanded equal total receipts at the start of the eighteen years, they are still equal at the end. But by the time the eighteen years are finished, our equal expenditures buy twice as many cars and only the same number of concerts, because the output of automobiles rises at a rate of 4 percent a year while the output of trio recitals remains constant. In Chapter 2, we noted an increase from 2.2 million to 11.3 million in the number of automobiles purchased by Americans, a move from one in fifteen to one in five in the proportion of American families that bought a new car—but the national income accounting over that generation actually showed a *decline* in the percentage of their income Americans spent for automobiles.

Let us change our Baumol-Bowen assumptions slightly and move 1 percent of the industrial work force to the service sector every year. Now the units of industrial production rise at a rate of 3 percent a year, while their prices continue steady; the units of service production rise at a rate of 1 percent a year, while their prices rise, still, at a rate of 4 percent. At the end of our eighteen years, we have a 70 percent increase in total industrial production, and a 20 percent increase in total services production; the price of each unit of industrial production is still the same, and the price of each unit of services production has doubled. Now, look at the dollar numbers, and assume that industrial and service sectors each commanded $100 million a year at the start of this process. By the end of it, the industrial sector (which has really grown 70 percent) will show a total income of $170 million, while the services sector (which has really grown only 20 percent) shows a total income of $242 million; from an economy where industrial production and service production showed equal shares, we will have moved to an economy where services represent 58 percent and goods only 42 percent of the gross national product as measured in money. Look at employment figures: where at the start of our very simple model, goods and services each employed the same numbers of people, the results after eighteen years show just under 60 percent employed in the service industries, just over 40 percent employed in the goods industries.

Clearly, if you look at the yardstick figures for "national product" and employment—the only figures anybody ever does look at—we have been moving from a goods-oriented to a services-oriented society. Everybody knows that's what has been happening in America: it is one of the universal clichés. *But it isn't true.* The truth is that our goods production has increased more than three times as much as our services production.

The famous "postindustrial society," in other words, simply is not so: it was all an accounting artifact. *The production of services, rather than becoming the leading force in the economy, has become a dragging force.* It is the services, not the goods, that "don't work right anymore." A threefold increase in postal rates produces fewer deliveries a week; a fourfold increase in the payroll at apartment houses produces automatic rather than manned elevators; a threefold increase in the per diem charge at nursing homes produces the failures of care that jump onto the front pages of the newspapers. New York City's income rises from $3.4 billion in 1964 to $12 billion in 1975—and the city slides into bankruptcy. The streets grow increasingly dirty; Mr. Kazin's library—and mine—goes into shock.

The service sector of the alleged service society becomes

increasingly like an underdeveloped country, where much is promised and little is delivered: our generation has a rendez-vous with fakery.

3

Imposed upon this already debilitating continuing change in cost ratios, inflation makes the problem psychologically unmanageable. The sense of correct ratios among prices, which people inherit from their childhood and early adulthood, is contaminated in everyone's memory by a lingering idea of "absolute" dollars-and-cents prices, which persists as a sort of partially erased magnetic blip in the human retrieval system. Sociologists like to say, meanly, that workers regard the wage increases they get through inflation as a reward for work and merit, while they regard the price increases as unjustified extortion.

Such "absolute" price signals may be triggered by extraordinary increases in prices for frequently purchased commodities (viz., beef in spring 1973, gasoline, heating oil, and electricity in early 1974, sugar in late 1974). In less frantic times, however, both the wages received and the prices paid for daily necessities move slowly enough to overprint specific price memories (though not ratios), and people are most unsettled by the motion of prices for things and services they buy only at widespread intervals. Thus increases in automobile and housing prices, while no greater than increases in other prices, are more widely publicized and resented, and produce greater consumer resistance, which reflects itself in the housing area in calls for rent controls and ceilings on mortgage interest rates. Thus, too, the special dangers to the economy in mandating expensive safety equipment and emission controls at a time when inflation is already escalating automobile prices.

Let us change the Baumol-Bowen arithmetic once again, and assume that the industrial workers, instead of accepting a 4 percent wage increase to match their increased productivity, demand and receive an 8 percent annual increase; and the service workers, with unchanging productivity, receive an identical raise. Then the prices of goods, under our assumptions, rise 4 percent a year; the prices of services rise 8 percent a year. At the end of eighteen years, the price of an automobile or a washing machine will have doubled in dollars and cents— and the price of a trio concert, a course in economics, a mail delivery or an obstetrical delivery will have quadrupled. People whose memories are imprinted with the prices of half a generation ago will be disturbed and frightened by the inflation in the price of goods; they will be appalled and terrified by the inflation in the price of services. Schematically, this is what we lived through in the early 1970s. The giant increases in the factor prices of raw materials and energy in 1973 and 1974 prevented, briefly, further deterioration in the ratios between the price of goods and the price of services: appalling and terrifying price increases were to be found everywhere. But with the return of inflation to more "manageable" levels, the influence of changing technology on relative prices will resume, to the detriment of government, education, medicine, craftsmanship, and the arts.

These forces are entirely man-made, and can be controlled by policy. What has prevented governments from dealing with the problem is in part the faulty analysis that leads economists and sociologists to proclaim the nonexistent shift from goods to services at the base of the economy, and in part a wrongheaded view of the function of politics.

The error in politics is the concentration on government action as a way to influence the distribution rather than the production of economic benefits. Our first question about tax or subsidy policy tends to be whether it is "fair" rather than whether it encourages or discourages over a period of time activities the society wishes to expand or limit.

When we make decisions about social security, unemployment insurance, and health maintenance programs, we never factor in the loss of incentive to save, though we understand well enough that increases in savings will be necessary if we are to create new jobs or police the environment without collapsing the economy. We spend more on the education of those whose schooling promises less return to the society from the effort, because they need help. We tax capital gains, impeding the flow of investment to emerging industries, because only fat cats benefit directly from such gains. Insistence on fairness often enough becomes a source of profits: if the oil industry gets a depletion allowance, as an encouragement to the risky activity of drilling, "justice" requires its extension to everyone else who can claim to be mining a dwindling resource—down to and including the workers of clam beds. Whether the purposes are noble or ignoble, the efficiencies are intolerably low.

This is the real advantage socialist societies enjoy today in their competition with capitalist societies: they understand that improvements in production are among the prime functions of government, and we have forgotten it. (Their distribution problem is solved by fiat: complaint is forbidden, and the fact that the most cherished goods of the society are allocated outside the pricing mechanism—adequate housing, automobiles, telephones, travel—means that officially reported income disparities, while still in fact high by the standards of modern capitalist societies, can be much lower than real income disparities.) Where we do consciously employ government policy to promote one activity rather than another—in housing programs and health programs, for example—we aim our shafts narrowly at specific goals, which often tends to make those goals unachievable because the prices rise so rapidly, and leaves us still at the mercy of the wider forces that produced the problem.

You can never change just one thing . . . Programs to assure the delivery of services at prices people are willing to pay will have to deal systemically with the differential impact of technology on different forms of economic activity. This is one area where I feel real confidence that I know what we ought to do, and the patient reader will find the answer in the back of the book. But I fear we are going to be a long time changing our *politique* to make it work, and today's aches and pains will grow to crippling dimensions before we seek out remedies.

5

... And Wastes

*The heavy plough and its consequence of distribution of
strips in the open fields helped to change the northern
peasants' attitude towards nature, and thus our own.
From time immemorial land was held by peasants in
allotments at least theoretically sufficient to support a
family. Although most peasants paid rent, usually in
produce and services, the assumption was subsistence
farming. Then in northern Europe, and there alone, the
heavy plough changed the basis of allotment: peasants
now held strips of land at least theoretically in
proportion to their contribution to the plough-team.
Thus the standard of land distribution ceased to be the
needs of a family and became the ability of a
power-engine to till the earth. No more fundamental
change in the idea of man's relation to the soil can be
imagined: once man had been part of nature; now he
became her exploiter.*

—*Lynn White,*
Medieval Technology and Social Change

1

Boiled down, the Baumol-Bowen dilemma states that under
conditions of improving technologies which apply unequally to
different sectors of the society, costs will change faster than
perceived values. A related theorem states the ecology
dilemma: under conditions of changing technology, real costs
will change faster than perceived costs.

A simple example is the introduction of tobacco harvesting machinery in the Carolinas, which will lower the price and the perceived costs of tobacco products—and load onto the streets of the struggling cities a new cadre of black farm laborers wretchedly incompetent to handle themselves or their environment in an urban setting. Accounting for and allocating such costs is a hard job, and nobody dreams of attempting it. Yet a rational calculus of the costs of growing tobacco in the 1980s should include at least some of the costs of urbanizing the displaced farm workers. Like the apparent shift from goods to services in the GNP, the declining relative cost of food products through the twenty-year period 1950–70 was at least in part an accounting artifact, because the costing system—we are back here to Milton Katz's "legal order," seen from a slightly different vantage point—did not load onto the price of food any of the expenses the cities had to undertake to keep the immigrant black farming community from self-destruction and to minimize the irritations its presence caused in the lives of others.

The problem of the immigrant black poor in the cities is essentially an *ecological* problem, though not usually seen as such. Let us take a look at a not dissimilar problem which everyone does see as environmental: the beef business, which reveals a visible drift through technological change, with the costs sloughed off to the environment.

Man was of necessity a herdsman before he was a farmer; and whenever in history land became cheaper than people (as in England in the fourteenth century, after the Black Death) an early result was the substitution of grazing for farming. But assuming that land can be farmed at all (which is not true, of course, for most of the earth's surface), agriculture will supplant grazing as soon as there are enough people to do the work. Barbed wire, that magnificent technology of the nineteenth century, makes the transition easier, but it will occur even in the absence of barbed wire. The transition points are the stuff of social crisis—the continuing wars between farmers and stockmen in the West, the enclosure movement in eighteenth-century England; and before those, indeed, the incessant border skirmishing and worse between the Byzantines and the Turks, the Russians and the Tartars.

In a well-ordered agricultural society, however, stock raising and farming work together. Cattle graze on the land left unfarmed in the rotation cycle, and their excrement fertilizes the fallow field. It is obviously folly to romanticize the life-style or the efficiency of the historic European peasant, to whom the adjective "brutish" was consistently and not unreasonably applied; but there is to us something satisfyingly harmonious about the natural processes by which animal life returned to the soil the chemical elements withdrawn from it in the growth of nutritive plants. Then guano broke the cycle; and soon we learned to synthesize and apply the chemicals required by the plants we wished to grow. The economic value of cattle excrement fell below the disutility of collecting it.

One step at a time: that's what makes trouble. While the cattle fattened on pastureland, the fact that it no longer paid to gather excrement had no public significance. But after World War II, agribusiness developed the feedlot as the cheapest procedure for producing beef: cattle raising became a form of farming, not herding. On grazing land, the "cow-calf ratio," the amount of land necessary to support a cow and her calf, was anywhere from three to four to forty acres per cow-calf. On feedlots, some dozens of steers can be kept on each acre, and fed on the grain from nearby farms. Their excrement now becomes a disposal problem.

No sooner said than done: put the feedlot on the banks of a river, and shovel the stuff in the water. With this disposal free of charge, the cost-efficiency of concentration in feedlots was overwhelming. By the end of the 1960s, the biological burden placed on American waterways by cattle excrement from feedlots was more than twice as great as the biological burden from the sewage systems of all the nation's cities. The feedlot here is merely a special case of the abuse by modern agriculture of the "free" water and air around the farm. Max Ways lamented that "the three-million high-technology U. S. farmers put more pressure on their land and rivers than the hundred-and-fifty million low-productivity peasant families of China put upon their land and rivers." Gerald Winfield in *The Annals of the American Academy of Political and Social Science* quantified the problem differently: "Agriculture produces 2,280 million tons of waste each year, an amount over nine times greater than the residential, commercial and industrial wastes combined."

The savings to cattle production from the use of this free disposal system ran into literally hundreds of millions of dollars a year; the costs to the outside world are essentially unmeasurable, because there is no marketplace, no system of valuation, to put a number on the deterioration of water quality. Meanwhile, further burdens are placed on the waterways by run-offs from the farms where partially poisonous inorganic chemical fertilizers have replaced the waste matter from domestic animals as the source of needed soil nutrients.

The problem is not unique to farming or to America. Most of the mussels, oysters, and scallops eaten in Europe come out of the tidal flats of the Wadden Sea, a branch of the North Sea adjoining northern Holland and Germany. Dredging for shellfish, the fishermen pull up great quantities of starfish. In the old days, this waste catch was sold to the farmers reclaiming the land behind the dikes; they need a great deal of fertilizer to vitalize their brackish soil. But now the chemicals have become cheaper, there is no market for dead starfish, and the fishermen simply dump them back into the water. The decaying mountains of dead starfish upset the balance of the tidal flat, diminishing shellfish production; and meanwhile the chemical substitutes leach out into the sea, helping the pesticides poison the shellfish beds.

It is traditional in American social criticism to attack our feedlot arrangements, with the highest degree of ferocity, as a giveaway to the cattle interests. A moment's thought about the Dutch and the starfish and the Wadden Sea should be proof enough that profits have nothing to do with it. So long as it is assumed that the waste-disposal system is cost-free, a socialist as much as a capitalist economy will seek the greater efficiency of the feedlot; and once the cost of waste disposal must be calculated, entrepreneurs can be made to pay that cost just as bureaucrats can—indeed, probably more easily. Given the highly competitive nature of the American cattle market, it is all but certain that the bulk of the apparent savings from free waste disposal is passed on to the community as a whole, in the form of lower beef prices. One cannot, then, "make the feedlot operator pay" for cleaning up the water: everybody must pay. This is what Walt Kelly was talking about when he said, "We have met the enemy and he is us."

Nobody ever made a *decision* to subsidize beef prices through polluted waterways: it was "natural." And such "natural" free goods are inevitably institutionalized through exploitation. We did make matters worse in the United States through unwise tax laws that further subsidized beef prices by making feedlots a tax dodge. (A rich man could buy "cattle"—actually shares in a cattle-buying venture—deduct the cost of their feed from his taxable income, and repeat the process as necessary to postpone tax payments, making the government an unseen partner in the venture. Assuming competition again, the net result was to reduce beef prices as well as to increase the post-tax income of rich investors.) Grain-fed, fatty beef commanded a premium from consumers, too. Fortunately, the jump in grain prices that followed the Russian wheat deal of 1972 made many feedlot operations uneconomic, many of the tax dodgers went broke, and for the first time since the war the proportion of cattle "finished" on remote grasslands rose.

(To the extent that the rest of the world still apes America, incidentally, this return to pasture would considerably improve life chances elsewhere. Through 1974 and 1975, guilt-ridden churchmen and editorial writers kept demanding that the rich cut down on grain-fed beef to release grain for the starving. But the few agronomists who could make their voices heard over this din were demonstrating that the most likely way to improve the protein intake of an expanding population was better

exploitation of the earth's vast grazing lands. It is also interesting to note that when the Russians made their big grain purchases in 1975, the fact that they wanted the corn to feed their
cattle went unremarked by all those who a year before had
been denouncing the American consumer's appetite for beef as
a cause of starvation in the poor countries. Humanitarian social
criticism tends to be highly selective.)

Unfortunately, the institutional structure in America has not
changed: the legal order as it affects the operation of feedlots
is much as it was a decade ago; and presumably as the grain
prices decline again the feedlots will come back into fashion.
Far from eliminating the ecologically damaging tax break for
feedlot operators, Congress in 1974 established a program to
guarantee the loans bankers had made to help the modern
cattle finishers acquire their stock.

2

Increasing populations at higher standards of living obviously
put pressure on the ecosphere; and where the other factors of
production become more expensive, technology tends to exploit to an increasing degree any air or water or urban facilities
that can be used for free. But it is by no means necessarily true
that technological change damages the physical environment.
The elimination of the great killer diseases and the reduction
of American infant mortality from 140 per thousand live births
in 1900 to 15 per thousand in 1970 must both be seen as *environmental* gains. So must the flood control projects around the
world, the afforestations of Israel, China, and Siberia, the irrigation works of the Imperial Valley and Libya and Iran. "The
introduction of technological devices, i.e., the growth of the
technosphere," says a British committee's *Blueprint for Survival*, ". . . can only occur to the detriment of the ecosphere,"
but they don't buttress that slogan with evidence; and, indeed,
it doesn't make sense.

The results of accelerated economic development since the

war are by no means entirely negative even in heavily industrialized areas. Improved sewage disposal has brought the sturgeon back to the Hudson for the first time in a century, bass back to the Hackensack River for the first time in a generation. The air over Pittsburgh, London, and Paris (to take only three) has improved beyond the imaginings of fifty years ago. Dark-walled cities with a romantic soft light as recently as the late 1950s, Paris and London became white cities with a northern sun after changes in heating technology eliminated what had been incredible quantities of particulate matter in the air. In London, the decade 1956–66 saw a 10 percent increase in population, a 17 percent increase in per capita energy consumption —and a 50 percent increase in the annual number of hours of sunshine.

Environmental degradation is not new, after all. Any archaeologist who has dug up a kitchen midden can testify that man has been making a junk heap of his surroundings from the days when he was numbered in the millions rather than the billions. Slash-and-burn agriculture devastated wide stretches of this continent in the days of the pioneers, and very ancient monuments survive in Mesopotamia to illustrate the destruction of water supplies that could be wrought by man in a state of primitive technology. Those who think pollution can be stopped by vows of poverty should take a whiff of Calcutta someday; the fact is that a degree of wealth is a necessary (clearly not a sufficient) condition for cleanliness.

The notion that nature is benign has always made better poetry than policy. Nature was making forest fires long before bears carried shovels and wore rangers' hats. At the top of Saarinen's glorious arch in St. Louis the tourist is invited to consider the current condition of the Mississippi, and informed that Lewis and Clark drank the water—but you wouldn't have wanted to drink the organic wastes in the muddy Mississippi at St. Louis at the time of Lewis and Clark or even earlier.

In America, the management of these problems is made infinitely more difficult by the manner of their presentation. Ecological apocalypse is forever upon us; great numbers of the young, the silly, and the literary march behind banners urging a return to the cave. Prizes are given to the somber expounders of the dreadful truth that Lake Erie is dead, fully eutrophied God save us, nothing can live in it; then we read that the mercury pollution scare has destroyed the livelihood of a thriving colony of commercial bass fishermen working the western shores of the lake—and nobody connects the two stories. The feedlots not only pollute the waterways: "the flatulence of domestic cattle," the *New York Times* solemnly reports, endangers the ozone layer of the atmosphere, which is being attacked by the methane rising from this source. (After reading this story, I made inquiry to find out whether someone was joking, and was rather sternly informed that Walter Sullivan, the *Times* science editor, never jokes. Especially, I guess, about the ozone layer, which he has also seen in jeopardy from supersonic aircraft and the freon in aerosol cans. Still, in my time of acquaintance with newspapers a city editor confronted with a story about the perilous flatulence of cattle would have sent his science editor first to the library to read up on the buffalo of the plains, and then to the zoo to watch the buffalo fart.) Our hunger for security, coupled with the middle-class American's guilty sense that things are too good to last, has made us infinitely credulous of disaster.

Among the examples of this credulity has been the vigorous revival of ancient worries that the weather is turning against human occupancy of the planet (a juicily satisfying worry because nothing can be done about it, if true), and that even if the weather holds, man will presently run out of key resources he needs to sustain his current patterns of life. "We are growing rich and numerous upon a source of wealth of which the fertility does not yet apparently decrease with our demands upon it," writes an eloquent if old-fashioned proponent of this view. "Hence the uniform and extraordinary rate of growth which this country presents. . . . But then I must point out the painful fact that such a rate of growth will before long rend our consumption of oil comparable with the total supply. In the increasing depth and difficulty of drilling we shall meet that vague, but inevitable boundary that will stop our progress. . . . A farm, however far pushed, will under proper cultivation continue to yield forever a constant crop. But in a well there is no reproduction and the produce once pushed to the utmost will soon begin to fail and sink to zero. So far, then, as our wealth and progress depend upon the superior command of oil, we must not only stop—we must go back."

That paragraph has been edited a bit, for the resource that William Stanley Jevons was worried about in 1865 was not oil but coal. Another difference was that nobody paid much attention to his book on this subject, while the Club of Rome got on the front pages in 1973 with a virtually identical statement. Keynes in 1936 suggested that "Jevons's . . . conclusions were influenced . . . by a psychological trait, unusually strong in him, which many other people share, a certain hoarding instinct, a readiness to be alarmed and excited by the idea of the exhaustion of resources. . . . Jevons held similar ideas as to the approaching scarcity of paper as a result of the vastness of the demand in relation to the supplies of suitable material. . . . Moreover, he acted on his fears and laid in such large stores not only of writing paper, but also of thin brown packing paper, that even today, more than fifty years after his death, his children have not used up the stock he left behind him of the latter."

The problem with the scarcity theories, as a number of critics have pointed out, is that they neglect the price/cost signals routinely uttered by the operation of the market. When oil prices were soaring, scientists went exploring the shale rocks in Colorado, the tar sands in Alberta and Venezuela, coal liquefaction possibilities, solar energy, wind power, laser-induced fusion, techniques for pumping water in to get oil out of oil wells, etc. There was money to be made that way, it seemed. If water runs short, it will become profitable for scientists and engineers to turn their attention to improving the efficiency of desalination machinery. As important minerals become scarce they become more expensive, and then technologies are refined until the exploitation of low-grade ore bodies produces metals at prices lower than those that prevailed when we were exploiting high-grade ore bodies. Substitutions proliferate, and what starts off cheaper often winds up better (i.e., nylon for silk); eventually recycling permits multiple reuse of scarce commodities—even undigested grain separated from cattle manure and fed back to the poor beasts.

Many of the false price/cost signals emitted by new technologies tend to be self-correcting. For technical reasons, the basic oxygen furnace cannot operate on cold steel scrap, and the initial impact of its introduction was to reduce the demand for scrap and create a pileup of ferrous junk around the world. But the increased pressure on the iron mines leads to increased prices for iron and the development of preheating techniques that return the recycling of scrap to the steelmaking process—even the derelict cars that were an eyesore on New York City streets got towed away by the scrap dealers. Feedlot proliferation drives up the cost of corn, reducing the previous savings from this mode of production, and returns an increasing proportion of the animals to grassland, at least temporarily. And there can be no question that the immense jump in the cost of energy in the mid-1970s, while artificially induced, is much better for the society than the 1960s belief in what Barbara Ward called "the incredible possibilities of unlimited energy." Our cars, our homes, our factories and office buildings will all be more efficient—and will represent less of a burden on the ecosphere—because the Arabs frightened us so in 1973, and robbed us so in the years that followed.

The application of cleverness to the problem of waste disposal has barely begun. Chicago dries its sewage sludge and sells it as fertilizer to Florida orange groves and to strip-miners restoring the soil. In Dusseldorf and in Paris, "water wall" incinerators burn dry garbage at high heat and generate steam for power plants. DuPage County in Illinois has built "Mount Trashmore," a 125-foot hill (the highest elevation in the county) atop the site of an old quarry, made of garbage cells separated and topped by clay; in the winter, it provides ski slopes and toboggan runs. (Munich did the same with the rubble left from the war.) A General Electric researcher has been breeding strains of bacteria that turn the two-thirds of urban garbage that is cellulose into a protein-rich animal feed; others are making both fuel and feed out of previously discarded straw. An eccentric Englishman has designed a little manure distillery that turns animal wastes into methane pure enough to run the engine he has designed for his automobile.

3

Among the most important functions of modern government— no doubt about it—is control over the damage to the environment from productive human activity. One cannot, however, stop people from exhaling in cities because the carbon dioxide they release may alter the composition of the air. Both strategies and tactics will have to be thought out considerably more carefully than the people in the environmental protection business have yet been willing to think.

There is a place for dedicated effluent taxes, of the kind that cleaned up the Ruhr half a century ago; there is room for general tax levies to build sewage facilities, like those that cleaned up Lake Washington in Seattle; there is room for indirect subsidy to private industry, like the tax exemptions on the pollution-control investment bonds of which American industry sold no less than $3 billion worth in 1974; there is even a small place for the sort of lawsuits Ralph Nader is forever initiating, though in general it is unwise to promote conflicts between "polluters" and "victims" if the goal is to protect society at large. For the problem is not pollution. "When you approach it in terms of pollution," Milton Katz told the House Committee on Science and Astronautics in 1969, "you are approaching it in terms of the symptoms. When you approach it in terms of technology assessment, you are going right to the source."

The difficulty is to find a proper time frame for the assessment of costs. The taconite industry in northern Minnesota rests on the investment of public moneys—raised through a bond issue approved by the state's voters—to create pelletizing plants that allow this low-grade ore to be processed into iron at a price competitive with that charged at those mines where the quality of the ore is better. The largest of these operations (it produces 10 percent of all the iron mined in the United States) dumps its "tailings," the discarded earth from the pelletizing process, into a very deep part of Lake Superior, where it was assumed that the heavy wastes would simply sink harmlessly to the bottom. But there are asbestos fibers in this earth, and they drift with the current to contaminate the water supply of Duluth, which is drawn from the lake. Asbestos in the air is unquestionably carcinogenic.

The company that operates the mine insists that the costs of dumping these huge quantities of slurried rock in the settling ponds suggested by the state government would in effect prevent the exploitation of the ore. The industry is there, and it has stockholders, employees, and customers not easily directed to other investments, jobs, and sources of supply. Today, the state would like to see the business closed down, but the Supreme Court eventually ruled that in the absence of proof that asbestos is in fact dangerous in drinking water the mining company cannot be expropriated from an investment originally made at the urging of the same state government that now demands its abandonment. Eventually, the mining company will have to find a new dump; but it must be permitted to keep producing while looking. Shortly after the Court ruled, a committee of the National Academy of Science decided that asbestos in drinking water probably does no harm. Now, what should who do next?

A bank executive in Phoenix observed sadly that the city really should have been built on the other side of Camelback, because where it stands is the best agricultural land in central Arizona—but, of course, that's why the pioneers settled in what became downtown Phoenix. The state of Pennsylvania is criss-crossed by uneconomic rail lines, which a national administration that wishes to make other use of tax revenues would like to close down—and a state administration that fears unemployment would like to see refurbished. It may (or may not) be that the costs of maintaining these rail lines, seen over a fifty-year period, are less than the costs of abandoning them and turning the traffic over to the trucks. We lack techniques not only to assess the reality of costs over an extended period, but even to decide how long a period should be considered. Keynes sourly observed that in the long run we are all dead; but contemporary man, so much more powerful, must not forget that his children's children will still be alive.

Except in rare situations like the landfills that threaten San Francisco Bay or the terrible diseconomies of strip-mining on slopes, it will be unwise policy to proceed by means of prohibitions and mandates. Deputy Administrator John Quarles of EPA told Paul Weaver of *Fortune* late in 1974, "Don't be so confident that what you don't know won't hurt you." He thought it was an argument for a free hand by his agency in enforcing its own ideas about how to protect the public, but it is of course an argument against detailed legislation and regulation. Certainly the EPA behaved recklessly in mandating the use of catalytic converters, which spew into the urban atmosphere small quantities of platinum oxides nobody has ever breathed—plus large quantities of sulfate oxides that are perhaps the most poisonous of all combustion pollutants, and never came out of automobile tailpipes before. EPA has been demanding that coal-burning power plants be equipped with scrubbers almost entirely for the purpose of reducing to near zero the quantity of sulfur dioxide emitted by that source—but if a quarter of the nation's automobiles were equipped with catalytic converters they would put into the air *at ground level* more sulfate oxide than all the scrubbers would remove from the air at smokestack level. Indeed, it isn't even certain that the sulfur dioxide emitted by the power plants becomes the much more poisonous sulfate oxide, which the catalytic converters unquestionably do emit.

The consequences of regulation as well as the consequences of pollution or poison must be taken into the equation. It now seems clear enough that both the power planners who said energy "requirements" would double in the 1970s and the ecologists who prevented the building of the Alaska pipeline and the siting of new nuclear plants were importantly wrong. "Regulatory bodies," as Harvey Brooks of Harvard told a House committee, "develop a prejudice against innovation. . . . They seldom give proper weight to the denial of benefits to society."

It is becoming increasingly likely that the complex of legislation which Congress passed to control drug research and new medications has done more harm than good. We know the horrors wrought by easy acceptance of thalidomide in Europe; what we can never know is the advances in drug therapy that have been foregone in reaction to those horrors. "It is entirely possible that if the ideal contraceptive were developed today, it would never be introduced in the United States," says Dr. Allan Barnes of the Rockefeller Foundation. ". . . A mood for absolute safety is sweeping the country. . . . We've begun to assume benefits and concentrate on risks. This is very dangerous to women and to research. . . ."

Victor Fuchs of Stanford observed that "penicillin and fluorexene, two valuable drugs, are both lethal to some laboratory animals. Thus if these drugs were just being developed today, the clear evidence of their toxicity in animals would probably result in their rejection long before approval was sought to market them. . . . FDA regulations are heavily biased in the direction of keeping drugs off the market. This is done in the name of saving lives (by preventing unsafe drugs from reaching the market) and saving money (by preventing inefficacious drugs from reaching the market). The net result, however, may be unnecessary suffering or even loss of life because some drugs that would be efficacious for some patients are not available."

In any event, despite the economists' learned talk of preventing "externalities"—costs of production that can be sloughed off to society as a whole rather than paid by the producer—it is essentially nonsense to say that we will "make the polluter pay." The consumer pays, because cost increases are passed on as price increases. Not infrequently, innocent third parties will have to pay costs "internalized" to the production process just as other innocent third parties paid when such costs were "externalized": costs do not fall so neatly in place as theoreticians believe. The use of investment moneys for pollution-control equipment rather than for increased production will boost unemployment and heighten inflation by reducing productivity; GNP in conventional measures will decline.

Obviously, the measures are wrong: a decrease in pollutants in the air is an economic value and should somehow be counted into the national product (or the production of bads deducted from the production of goods; somebody once suggested the creation of a GNE, or Gross National Effluent, to be deducted from GNP). But we must face the fact that wealth is being transferred from people who don't live near the source of the pollutant (but must pay the increased prices and suffer the effects of economic decline) to people who do. And we must also come to grips with the fact that the very large investments needed for pollution control (and for occupational safety, which is a related consideration) will be possible only for large enterprises; one cannot honestly assert the primacy of both the anti-trust laws and the environmental protection laws. Finally, like all technological change, the development of pollution-reducing capacity will distort the relationship of prices and perceived value in the market.

Politically, over the long haul, a failure to face up to these transfer effects will be fatal to the environmental movement, and maybe to the environment. A political process that accepts (or consciously lies about) the fact that all change produces losers as well as winners will have to be developed if we are to meet Ralph Lapp's demand for "a Triple-E statement that strikes a balance between environmental, economic and energy considerations."

How we get from here to there is subject matter for the last chapters of this book, but there is a dragon in the path that should be noted at once: the legitimation of scare tactics in political debate about environmental issues. At the 1975 meeting of the American Association for the Advancement of Science, chemist Mary Good estimated that radioactive emissions from the nuclear energy installations proposed for the year 2000 would increase the estimated cancer deaths in America by almost nine persons per year. The comparison for the average citizen would be the risk of going a fraction of an ounce overweight, or smoking 0.03 cigarettes a year, or driving one mile in a car. But "one unnecessary death is too many"—and some Concerned Scientist could (does) command headlines by proclaiming that the estimate is a hundred times too low (comparable, say, to the risk of smoking three cigarettes a year or driving a hundred miles in a car). Twenty years of experience with literally hundreds of nuclear power plants in the United States and Europe have yet to produce a death from an operating unit, yet the newspapers have managed to convince most of the country that the procedure is extremely hazardous. (The argument that nuclear plants increase society's susceptibility to sabotage should be accepted only from people who are also opposed to public water-supply systems.) And the shortage of power production from nuclear plants in 1980, as against what was expected from such installations when the decade started, will require the importation of an additional million barrels of oil every day, the dangers of which (including pollution of the sea from tanker mishaps) are demonstrably real.

Fashions change: the little old ladies in tennis sneakers who opposed the fluoridation of water supplies in the 1950s have become doughty warriors for the environment in the 1970s. Soon they will again look less heroic, for there are cycles in the attitude toward science and technology as in everything else. But with the improvement in communication techniques and the increasing use of "news" to satisfy the demand for entertainment, we lose the intelligent bias toward the statistical that characterizes both economic and political procedure at their best. The news media and (as we shall see) the courts become increasingly important, and both particularize the problems with which they deal. Because the world is in truth statistical and not particular—a truth we find hard to accept, each individual's view being inescapably particular—the result of excessive concentration on individual cases tends to be a spreading irrationality.

Electric heating is by far the most wasteful way to keep a house warm in winter: it involves turning heat to electricity, losing electrical energy in the transmission system, and then making heat from what remains of the electricity. Yet in early 1975, when energy conservation was one of the rallying points of government, the Public Service Commission in New York State ordered that state's public utilities to reduce their charges to electrically heated homes and make up the losses by charging more to oil- and gas-heated homes. A dissenting member of the commission noted sourly that it was like making Volkswagen owners pay more for gasoline so Cadillac owners could buy it cheaper, and he was right; but in particular terms, the burden on owners of electrically heated homes had grown too heavy to be borne.

Such irrational decisions will become increasingly common—and increasingly significant—in the years ahead. Experience, Oscar Wilde observed, is the name we give to our past mistakes; policy, economist Henry Wallich added, is the name we give to our future mistakes. What we lack is a systemic understanding of the consequences of deliberate decision. But government is increasingly and in part correctly committed to the frustration of the markets that work out these consequences; and the political process required to weigh a multiplicity of consequences is not even within our sight, let alone within our grasp.

6

A Shrinking World

Gov. Pires [of Portuguese Timor] would like to develop a meat industry for export—there are tens of thousands of head of buffalo and the Balinese cow here—but since these are considered wealth and are particularly valuable when young men have to pay the "bride price" to the family of their girl, natives are reluctant to slaughter until long past the time the meat is any good.

—Wall Street Journal

1

Nearly everyone agrees that a major cause of the dervish dance of inflation that whirled through all the nations of the West in the early 1970s was the unique coordination of their prosperity. It was something new in the world. Though climatic change or epidemic could rapidly alter the fate of large sections of the globe, different regions had tended historically to do well at different times. Indeed, the "terms of trade," the changing comparative values of different commodities and manufactured goods, virtually guaranteed that economic developments would make losers while they made winners. If Baltic and American grain boosted the prosperity of Lancashire, it depressed the towns of the Ile de France.

Mostly, though, economies and societies were insulated from each other. Before the nineteenth century, regions within a single country tended to be highly self-sufficient. The great accomplishment of the nineteenth century was the creation of the unified nation-state, studied in school as the story of Germany and Italy but really equally true everywhere, regardless of the stability or fragility of political forms.

In America, the historians and political scientists say that the confederal system of government devised by the Founding Fathers was destroyed by the Civil War. The end of that trauma found us newly supplied with a national paper currency and nationally chartered banks, a basic political issue ("the bloody shirt") that united the dominant North behind a single political party for half a century, and the constitutional high ground of the Fourteenth Amendment, on which for more than a generation a conservative Supreme Court stood guard against social or political experimentation by the states.

The economist sees it otherwise: for him, the great nationalizing force was the railroad, which ultimately created national markets for goods, capital, and labor, and nationwide organizations for getting and spending. (Note in this connection the interdependence of technologies: James E. Webb, who ran NASA, has pointed out that national or even regional coordination of rail service would have been impossible before the telegraph was invented, giving dispatchers the chance to move trains around on remote tracks.) Railroad-made markets and organizations in turn called forth national magazines and Daniel Boorstin's "statistical communities" of Americans who live in different places and do not know each other but are similarly situated to such an extent that their response to common stimuli will be much alike. Then the trend lines were given hyperbolic acceleration by radio, television, and the interstate highway system. The states themselves, theoretically sovereign, became irrelevant.

Next: Charles Kindleberger sees "the jet aircraft and the international firm . . . preparing the same fate for the nation-state." He could also have mentioned the communications satellite, the common languages of data processing, and the unbelievable growth of international communications (a volume that doubles every four years or so) occasioned by these two factors.

Under the eye of eternity, what we are talking about is probably the same thing Henry Luce used to call "the American Century." The cultural trends that are in process of diffusion around the globe are predominantly American: though Fiat rather than Ford may actually be building the Soviet automobile manufacturing capacity, it is Henry Ford's idea that supports the structure. (And the Russians wanted Ford, but in those days the American government—it was Kennedy's government—would not let Ford go out to play.) Multinational corporations in consumer goods businesses, which fifteen years ago hired anthropologists to advise them on the presentation of new products to culturally disparate societies, now simply turn the problem over to an international advertising agency, which runs the same campaign at the same time all over the world. This is not entirely new, either—Harry Kramer, who owned a proprietary laxative called Cascarets, once told his young advertising agent, "Mr. Wasey, the whole world is constipated." But it's only recently that all of Europe could be urged to put a tiger in its tank, or place itself in the good hands of Allstate, or join the Pepsi generation.

Pockets of romantic resistance survive, as the ethnicity boom demonstrates. The ardent young find miracles in places like Cuba (where there are "free" telephone calls, as though the people who work in the telephone system did not have to be paid); and it is not impossible that the Chinese will find some entirely different organizational pattern to defeat the culturally barren logic of market economics. But attempts in the West to break the mold have been disastrous. In America itself the so-called counterculture sank to earth in the maze of its own contradictions. And in Europe the last-ditch struggle of Charles de Gaulle to maintain an overriding reverence for older values collapsed in the strikes of spring 1968—generally regarded as a "student revolt" because the students made the noise, but in fact the triumph of Gompers-style unionism on the home ground of Sorel-style unionism, a successful demand by French workers for their share of the consumer society. This worked so well, incidentally, that by 1973 Herman Kahn was suggesting that the home of Montaigne and Molière might become the Japan of the West before the year 2000. Of course, the conquest of other cultures by American technology spawned violent anti-Americanism, and nowhere more so than in France. *Tant pis.*

2

History is not what Gibbon thought it was: the record of the crimes and follies of mankind. It is, instead, the story of cultural diffusion, of the influence of communities on their neighbors. The influence was rarely exerted (rarity made it history), and usually it was exerted by fire and sword, by the eruption of the Roman legions from southern Italy, or the Mongol and Turkic horsemen from central Asia, or the Arab fanatics from the sands of the Middle East, or the Russians from Muscovy. But there have also been conquests of ideas: Christianity in Europe, Buddhism briefly in China and Japan, the French creation of bourgeois civilization under the patronage of Louis XIV. Every civilized person, it used to be said, had two homelands, and one of them was France. We are now far enough beyond the end of the British Empire to see that the center of that successful imperialism was the appeal of the English model to the aristocracies of the countries it invaded, that the admiration of local leadership for the qualities of the English gentleman was far more important than British armed force in maintaining for the better part of a century the viability of rule from London.

What has happened in the American century is rather different, much better encompassed under the rubric "technology transfer" than under the category "imperialism." One must insist, again, that such transfers are not original to our times. Geoffrey Bibby paints a picture of "the superb flintsmiths of Denmark" copying "the bronze daggers and spearheads of the south, in copper-colored flint, flaking the stone to the thinness of the metal prototype"—in 1650 BC. Lynn White and Fernand Braudel have shown how quickly a new technique could spread all across the Eurasian continent as early as the ninth and tenth centuries AD. Conventional history tells the story of the introduction of the horse to the American continent, and of the potato to Ireland and Germany. Moreover, the culture America has diffused is ideationally not original; indeed, the efficiency with which America has spread its *geist* around the world has been possible because the ground was prepared. American attitudes are essentially an imitative extension of the great thrust from Europe that began more than six hundred years ago.

We start with the clock. "Why didn't the clock remain a toy?" Sebastian de Grazia asked despairingly a decade ago. "Why didn't it delight or fascinate a few people and stop right there?" Because "the clock . . . provided the means whereby large-scale industry could coordinate the movements of men and materials to the regularity of machines. . . . The clock's presence everywhere, and its tie to the factory with its relatively unskilled work, soon gave rise to the idea that one was selling time as well as, or rather than, skill." That is all pre-American; but the full adjustment to the consequences is an American development. Until quite recently, punctuality was considered in Europe to be an American vice. " 'I'll see you at 4:10, then,' " de Grazia grumbles, "is a sentence that would have been comprehensible to no other civilization this earth has seen."

Efficiency in the division of labor requires intricate and precise synchronization and sequencing, and the results are measurable, which means that production planning continually improves through trial and error. (Then the prestige of precisely timed production planning is transferred to policy planning, where the results are not measurable and improvements are to a large extent a matter of luck.) Among the subsidiary techniques developed to new levels of effectiveness is the procedure for spreading innovation quickly through a society and across borders. Consumer innovations are of course the most noticeable—Coca-Colonization and the like—but what happens in the infrastructure of production is far more significant. In industrial production in recent years, we have had computerized machine tools, new fasteners and glues, containerized shipping, reinforced concrete technology and the Danish crane that lifts itself by its bootstraps, basic oxygen steel processes, random-access disc storage and time-sharing, supertankers, surveying by laser and by infrared photography, heat switches and much, much else, all universally adopted in modern societies.

Much of this could have happened and to a degree did happen in the British century, a hundred years ago. What our century has contributed as idea and as reality is a new relationship between speed and time. Telecommunications especially is the great controller of time: the telephone imposes one man's time-preference schedules on another; the radio and television schedules are inviolate, and the nature of the experience shared by the audience rests on the assertion that time is the same for all of them. The Egyptians had no commonly employed word for "minute," the Romans had none for "second." In an age of space travel and computers, we need not just "milliseconds," but "nanoseconds." *Sequence* is the absolute of the modern world; our lives are measured out by the infinitesimal quanta of Zacharias's atomic clock.

3

The central importance of telecommunications is its virtually instantaneous delivery of major price/cost signals to all parts of the world. Inevitably, the impact is greatest when the "international trade" involved consists of the moving about of book entries in computer storage. Currency exchange rates are now identical all over the world, simply because once a man can get more francs for dollars in New York than he can in Paris he will keep the telephone line open—buying francs in New York and selling them in Paris and pocketing the difference—until the prices equilibrate.

In theory, currency markets cannot get too seriously out of whack, because paper money is really part of each country's

national debt and the central banks can conveniently intervene, manufacturing money at will, to keep prices from moving
too fast. In fact, however, the possibilities for virtually instantaneous recycling may produce dizzying instability at moments
of crisis. In February 1973, for example, there was a gush of
feeling that the dollar, already twice devalued, would have to
be devalued again. It was a lunatic feeling—if anything, the
second devaluation of the dollar had brought it below its true
purchasing power (i.e., the amount of real goods that could be
purchased with a dollar in America was greater than the
amount of real goods that could be purchased with the ex-
change-rate equivalent of European currencies in Europe). But
a dozen years of mounting U.S. balance-of-payments deficits
had piled up immense quantities of dollars (Eurodollars) abroad,
and people who had twice seen their holdings of dollars sud-
denly lose value were quite willing to believe that it was about
to happen a third time. They descended on the Bundesbank to
buy German marks at the official exchange rate; and the German government, feeling committed to maintain that exchange
rate, in effect printed new marks and sold them for dollars.

The dollars the Bundesbank had acquired were now available
for investment in the only place they really could be invested,
which was the United States; and the Bundesbank cabled its
opposite number in America, the Federal Reserve Bank, to
purchase government securities for the German account. As
the Fed bought Treasury bills in the open market, however, it
created new reserves for the American banks, and there were
customers waiting in line to borrow those new dollars for the
purpose of shipping them to Germany, where they could be
used to buy marks. A morning of this nonsense produced a
leakage of almost $3 billion from dollars into marks; and the
Germans shut down the currency exchange system for—as it
turned out—more than two weeks.

What had happened here was a loss of the old frictional devices that had kept even the worst currency panics from accelerating beyond a certain speed. In the nineteenth century,

international accounts were settled by the exchange of gold bullion, which took considerable time to take out of vaults and load onto ships. If fundamental adjustments in exchange rates were required, there was time to make them before all the gold drained away; if they were not required, there was time to mobilize defenses against speculators. Moreover, because the system assumed internal friction, the sudden application of the brakes represented by a suspension of the market was not considered such a horror. The Russian announcement of general mobilization of July 29, 1914, closed every stock market in Europe; and two days later, on July 31, the New York Stock Exchange closed. The New York market did not reopen until late in November, and then only for bond trading; even restricted trading in stocks did not resume until mid-December. Today there is hell to pay if even a day is lost, and the collapse of the currency exchanges in early 1973 was traumatic. When they reopened, as "free" markets where currencies would seek their own level instead of trading at "official" prices, the dollar steadily lost another 20 percent of its value in terms of the stronger European currencies and the Japanese yen—which meant, from an American consumer's point of view, that the first 20 percent rise in his food prices was in fact no price increase at all for foreign customers buying American commodities. Maybe it's a good thing the average American doesn't understand what goes on in the financial markets.

For the fluctuations of currencies are only part of the danger of worldwide markets linked by almost instant telecommunications. Where the book entries that can be traded over the wire represent known quantities of private assets—shares of stock and commodity futures—the oscillations that can be created by the speed of international transaction may directly influence consumer prices and production planning in almost every branch of industry. The proximate cause of the worldwide inflation of 1973–74 was competitive stockpiling of commodities by manufacturers and others hoping to insulate themselves from the vagaries of wildly fluctuating markets (and then much of the recession of 1974–75 was caused by the running down of these stockpiles). Today information exchange over vast distances is better than information exchange in one place, and the uniformity of worldwide wholesale markets is actually greater than the unity of markets within a neighborhood. In 1974, when there were differences of 20 percent between the price of gasoline at the pump in adjacent boroughs of New York City, there was never more than 2 percent separating the price of a barrel of equivalent oil with its tankerage in Kuwait, Indonesia, Nigeria, and Venezuela.

Telecommunications also of course vastly increase the nation-state's capacity to act or react at a distance. Psychologist Charles Ramond recently amused himself with the chronology of the calling of the First Continental Congress—proposed by the Massachusetts House of Representatives on June 17, 1774, to meet in Philadelphia on September 1 (the earliest feasible date). "The meeting remained in session off and on until April 14, 1775, when General Gage finally received orders from England to arrest the rebels. It is interesting to speculate whether our country would have been founded if Gage could have telephoned London for guidance ten months earlier. . . ." At the same time, however, the fact of immediate communications outward limits substantially what a nation-state can do in seeking to influence its domestic economy. The danger that dollars would leak out to earn higher interest rates in Europe, producing further devaluation and resulting pressure on the prices of American commodities, was a fundamental constraint on the pump-priming the Federal Reserve could do in its efforts to speed up the flow of business in the United States in early 1975.

As late as 1932, Herbert Hoover could say that the U.S. tariff was "solely a domestic question." By the 1970s, governments had to face the fact that even their domestic tax and manpower policies could not be considered without reference to international flows of production factors—men and machines as well as finance capital. Henry Kissinger as a professor of political science had always expressed scorn for economic factors as an explanation of historical events. In 1971, when the dollar was first devalued, he found the foreign policy he had been developing with Richard Nixon lying in ruins all around him, and he called the British Ambassador (who happened to be Lord Cromer of the Baring family, a former governor of the Bank of England) to solicit an immediate personal cram course in international money and banking. By 1975, Kissinger was insisting that international considerations had to be primary in the development of American energy policy, and Paul Samuelson was suggesting not very respectfully that the "boy economist" leave the formulation of economic policies to those with a deeper background in the subject. But it was no longer possible for a Secretary of State to accept domestic economic policy as a given.

4

Visibly, the heart of cultural diffusion from America to the rest of the world is the automobile. No product of twentieth-century technology has given so much pleasure to so many people or lies so close to the heart of the values virtually everyone in a democracy professes. "Each man at the wheel," Roger Starr writes, "is master of his own destiny, captain of his own soul. On an objective scale it may be ridiculous that anyone should be reduced to inflating his *amour propre* by sitting at the wheel of an automobile wedged into a mass of other stalled machines. At the wheel of each sits another man feeling equally self-determined. But the absurdity makes the feeling no less real; on the contrary, the absurdity merely emphasizes how few are the occasions in modern life when one has the opportunity to exercise that individual control and individual choice which the philosophers of democracy and the sellers of soap agree are the most important attributes of free men. . . . The automobile . . . satisfies what is simultaneously an economic necessity and a profound psychological need—an instrument, one of the few, which man controls himself, and in whose design he takes pride."

Amen. American cars are by universal agreement too big and too wasteful, but to the extent that the current critics are attacking the automobile itself they do not know what they are talking about; and if they insist on tying other things they care about to their crusade against the car, they will lose all. The experiential content of the word "liberation" even for the Americans who use it is the first moment of possession of a driver's license and access to a car. Even today, against all the pressures of propaganda, it is the most visibly joyful and pride-provoking rite of passage in American society: high school graduation cannot hold a candle to it. Half-jokingly (only half) it can be said that the animal was not created to walk on two feet, has never liked it, and was thus from the beginning a sucker for any device that could get him from one place to another without walking. The great equestrian statues of antiquity reveal the power of the idea of transportation that does not depend on one's own muscles; the automobile perfects that idea. There is no freedom like "having wheels."

"A highly developed transport and communications system," writes E. S. Schumacher, the inheritor of the long English tradition of the simple-social-lifer, "has one immensely powerful effect: it makes people *footloose.*" But this footlooseness is what ordinary men mean by freedom, as even Schumacher eventually must concede—it does "open up a new dimension of freedom . . . in some rather trivial respects." But then he pulls himself together: "These achievements," he decides, "also tend to destroy freedom, by making everything extremely vulnerable and extremely insecure." Some vulnerability and insecurity have always been the price of freedom; there is no freedom without them. And in this instance the observation is wrong: affluence brings redundancy, which makes the individual's world much less vulnerable to minor disaster than ever before. In DeSica's movie, a bicycle thief can destroy the hopes of a family; in today's America, the insurance company pays for a rental car when the automobile thief absconds with the vehicle—and the family probably has a second car, anyway.

In any event, the appeal of the automobile is universal. Hitler was among the first European political leaders to understand it: he promised the Germans a Volkswagen. Europe in the years right after the war was too poor for cars; and the Italians began their economic miracle by inventing the motor scooter, the workingman's wheels. Movies survive to show how important the scooter was as a symbol of self-esteem for the young Europeans of the 1950s. But the car offers privacy, greater comfort, and speed (not to mention protection from the weather), and when the economies grew to the point where they could support the mass production of automobiles, Europe followed the American model. So did Eastern Europe. (I have long felt that what really brought the Politburo to dismiss Khrushchev was his opposition to the Fiat factory: in his dictated memoirs he was still fighting "to put the interests of millions who want to be well fed above the interests of thousands who will get pleasure out of buying a Fiat. That's my view. Unfortunately, I'm not in the leadership, and the new leadership either has a different perception of the situation or has lost touch with the true state of affairs." His place was taken by the car nut Leonid Brezhnev.) The first big purchase the Arabs tried to make with their money was Daimler-Benz, which makes the Mercedes.

For those who knew Europe as tourists in the 1950s, the deluge of automobiles in city and country is surely the greatest single change of the last fifteen years. Americans don't like to see it: it's too much like what they left home to get away from. Moreover, though they are not conscious of this source of their resentment, they find their own status in Europe much diminished; America was first and foremost the land where ordinary people had cars, which was then a wonder and is now not such a much. Underneath what the tourists see, of course, the changes are more profound, in patterns of land use, social organization, holiday, political issues (the communists in Paris have been the fiercest fighters against the imposition of substantial fines for illegal parking), and especially family life. For the automobile, like the television set, brings families together for experiences that once divided them—and sets up the nuclear unit in its automobile separated from the rest of the world. Some of the strength technology took from the family by the reorganization of work it gives back in leisure time.

Other social developments associated with the automobile are profoundly troubling, and seem to be as universal as the lust for the instrument. One of the most striking changes of the last fifty years has been the residential segregation of rich from poor. Jonathan Rubinstein has traced this tendency back to the eighteenth century and the first eruptions of uncontrollable street crime, stimulated by addiction to gin; René Dubos has placed it in the nineteenth century, and attributed it to the fear of infection in epidemics. But the fact is that as late as the second decade of this century city neighborhoods were more likely to be segregated by ethnic group than by income, and were likely to contain from within each ethnic group a mixture of upper middle class, middle class, and poor. Some neighborhoods in the older cities—New York, Boston, Philadelphia, Chicago, San Francisco, New Orleans—still do. With the arrival of the automobile, residential segregation by social class became the norm, first in the United States and then increasingly elsewhere. Racial conflict tells part of the story, but only part. Suburbanization, the growth of satellite centers, the isolation of the poor, a felt need to redefine the idea of a city—all these have come with the automobile to Milan as well as to Houston, to Tokyo as well as to Seattle. The betting here is that East Berlin and Warsaw and Kiev will not escape, for the automobile vastly increases the possibility of spatial choice, and people who otherwise live in rather different ways seem to exploit such possibilities in similar ways.

Another change related to improvements in transportation has come in the nature of immigration to metropolis. There is nothing new about a city importing strangers to do its dirty work. Braudel quotes a report about Paris in 1788: "The people known as common laborers are almost all foreigners. The Savo-

yards are decorators, floor polishers and sawyers; the Avergnats
. . . almost all water-carriers; the natives of Limousin are ma-
sons; the Lyonese are generally porters and chair-carriers; the
Normans, stone-cutters, pavers and pedlars, menders of crock-
ery, rabbit-skin merchants. . . ." Emma Lazarus was uncharita-
ble but surely not far off the mark in her poetic description of
those who sailed past the Statue of Liberty. But the immense
influx of Mediterranean laborers to northern Europe—and of
Puerto Ricans to northern United States—has been unique in
history, because most of these workers expect to go home after
a specified tour. The numbers have been startling. More than
10 percent of the total available male work force of Greek,
Algerian, Yugoslav, and Portuguese nationality was working in
France, Germany, and the Benelux countries in 1971; and if one
includes Italia Settentrionale as part of northern Europe at least
a quarter of the working population of southern Italy had gone
north. It is a circulating group: to gain a net increase of fifty
thousand Puerto Ricans in New York, the odds are that 250,000
will have to arrive, because 200,000 will return to warmer cli-
mates.

Because of their expectation of transiency, these new immigrants form a far more indigestible mass in the modern city
than even the immigrants of the past—who God knows had it
hard enough. They are mostly detested by the permanent
population, partly because of the prejudice in all societies
against foreigners, partly for the classic reasons of caste—those
who do the jobs others don't wish to do tend to have low status
in any society. Their presence slows what would otherwise be
a healthy social tendency to pay people more to compensate for
the nastiness of the work they do (the presence of large numbers of low-skilled Negroes acts as a brake on this tendency in
the United States, especially in the South). And when they return to their homelands, the effect of the skills, attitudes, and
tastes that are part of their baggage seems to be extraordinarily
complicated.

Returned workers have learned about the clock, which is

invaluable, and they have acquired the sense that life can be more *interesting* than they had previously realized. ("How ya gonna keep them down on the farm/ After they've seen Pareee?") But they have also adopted ideologies that are not really very useful even in the places where they were acquired and are wholly tangential to the problems of the home country —and they have acquired expensive consumer habits. Several studies have indicated that the balance-of-payments gains from remittances sent home by subsequent generations of Greek and Portuguese workers in northern Europe are more than eaten up by the increase in importation of northern European goods demanded by those who have already returned. The contrast between the needs of the society and this externally induced demand by a leading group distorts the economic market in poor Mediterranean countries and makes government planning an even worse mess than usual.

5

Cultural diffusion is a process that has winners and losers. To this point, we have been talking about winners, for the countries on the northern shore of the Mediterranean are all culturally viable. But a large proportion of the world's population is trapped in a cultural heritage that cannot be adapted to present or future conditions. Thus Athens itself died, and Nineveh and Tyre, the Amerindians who came in contact with measles-bearing Europeans, the Toltec as human sacrifices for the Aztec, the Roman Syrians in the age of the Huns: "The East has been carried into captivity," wrote Cyrillonas, "and nobody lives in the destroyed cities. . . . If the Huns will conquer me, Oh Lord, why have I taken refuge with the holy martyrs? If their swords kill my sons, why did I embrace Thine exalted cross?" It happens. Read the Bible.

But the weapon with which modern societies destroyed conflicting cultures was a peculiarly horrible one: public health.

"The incursion of Western medicine," Robert Heilbroner wrote in *The Great Ascent,* while he still considered himself an optimist, "has broken an age-old balance of population and productivity, and precipitated a situation in which not stasis but deterioration is the terrible fate which stares nearly every backward country in the face. From the relentless, crushing increments of population there is no escape, short of plague and mass death, other than a swift ascent to a new level of industrial provisioning." To Europe, public health came last, after the industrial revolution had established the conditions for an economic growth that could outdistance the propensity to multiply, and social conditions had created cyclical rather than endlessly progressive tendencies in the birthrate. To the "developing countries" public health came first, in the form of cheap antibiotics and insecticides. . . . You can never change just one thing.

Modernism has been imposed by public health on societies that never knew the clock, without thought that all division of labor rests on the premise of a common clock. The breakup of traditional modes of production undermines family and tribal loyalties, and people leak off the land to the cities created by the colonial powers as entrepots—cities that, as the U.N. Committee on Housing put it, "did not grow up, like the cities of Europe and North America, in the wake of local diversification and sustained development. They were, in a real sense, larger than and ahead of the economy sustaining them." The result has been what William J. Barber has called "an extreme case of 'parasitic' urbanization . . . swollen by refugees from rural distress."

We have sliced into a spiral of decline and must follow it downward. Government is in the cities: among the parasites are the elite. For reasons that run the gamut from charity through commitment to fear, they frame their policies first to mitigate the condition of the wretched city dwellers. The result is the vicious circle that can be observed in nearly all the tropical countries: food prices are controlled to keep the city dwellers placid, diminishing the incentive for farmers to produce and for people to stay on the farms; meanwhile, low farm prices mean that the farmers cannot become significant markets for industrial output from the cities, which must be oriented toward export or toward luxury products for the parasitical elite. In most developing countries, this is called "socialism."

Different growth rates in different geographic, ethnic, or class sectors of the society are discouraged as inequitable, though nothing is more obvious than the fact that every society must always have leading and lagging sectors. Punjab has doubled grain production; Uttar Pradesh has gone downhill; the government of India therefore restricts the Punjab's access to resources to assure greater supplies for the less efficient Uttar Pradesh. Progressive taxation and factory legislation are imported from modern societies without question, though the first encourages investment in invisible assets (or foreign assets) rather than in plant and equipment, while the second penalizes larger, more efficient operations and encourages what Stanislaw Wellisz calls "the persistence of small, antiquated shops that are exempt from the legislation. Many of the social laws have important objectives that cannot be neglected," he continues, "but these objectives must be pursued by means that are not inimical to technological and economic progress, lest they be self-defeating."

In the end, *all* innovation and entrepreneurship are discouraged, partly because the members of the one-party state fear any source of wealth other than the government, partly because of what P. T. Bauer has called "the antipathy of the British-trained type of civil servant, literate and 'responsible,' to the semi-literate and socially unacceptable type of individual who possesses the knack of making money by trading." There were good reasons why Marx saw socialism arriving only after the bourgeois tasks of development were complete. In the tropical countries today, planning is attempted without the statistical base that makes such activities plausible (let alone functional); capital creation proceeds by fiat without reference to the market that is to be served; and everybody lies to everybody else about what is being accomplished. Many of the best-trained of the leadership cadres emigrate, and become citizens of other countries or permanent "students" who pretend to be plotting revolutions for the homelands they have abandoned.

The exceptions are marked by more or less brutal exploitation by outsiders of the one resource an urbanized underdeveloped society offers: quantities of unskilled but intelligent labor. In Korea, Taiwan, Singapore, Hong Kong, Malaysia, Ivory Coast, and a few others, multinational corporations organize the modernized sector of the economy to gain the benefits of a largely female work force prepared to perform repetitive activities for long days at low wages. The employment of women is crucial, because it eliminates the horror of urbanization in Africa and part of South America, the tendency of men to flock to the cities while the womenfolk stay home and do not till the fields. And the firm intrusion of the cash-and-clock economy seems to create ripple effects that make the cities of these more successful countries more like the fruitful hellholes of nineteenth-century Europe than like the dying sewers of twentieth-century Africa and India.

The value of communism to these societies is its efficiency in making people go to one place and stay there. Nobody moves without official authorization: your identity card gives you identity (and, more serious, food rations) in only one place. The Russians can build the mineral and industrial wealth of Siberia with slave labor from the concentration camps; the Chinese can send fresh blood from the urban schools out to the peasant villages. Khrushchev was forever worrying about the fact that it takes 55 percent of the Russian population to feed the country not very well while 4 percent of the population produce food surpluses in America; but from the point of view of the tropical countries this inefficiency is if anything an advantage. The cheap resource for them is people. Their need is not to maximize the productivity of individuals (and thus their "worth") by supporting their efforts lavishly with land and capital; it is to maximize the productivity of land or capital by lavishly support-ing it with people. This is not Marxism or socialism; but it does have operational value to the homelands of the poor.

The one thing that certainly will not work is the collection of childish attitudes huddled together under the rubric of the Third World. The inherited cultures of tropical poverty can offer no models that will avert catastrophe in conditions of continually expanding population. The deaths of hundreds of millions of human beings will blight the consciences of the well-meaning western scholars and churchmen who espoused cultural relativism at a time when the most urgent need and the hardest task was for drastic cultural change. The moral superi-ority or inferiority of cultures was never an issue; nothing mat-tered but cultural adaptability to the aftermath of public health. Yet the commitment to cultural relativism grew so strong that even the occasional elements of a foreign culture totally inde-fensible by *moral* standards acquired their loyal supporters: in a review published in early 1975, Diana Tonsich of the Univer-sity of Pennsylvania went tsk-tsk at the memory of Lord Wil-liam Bentinck, who as governor-general of India abolished the custom of *suttee* (the self-immolation of widows on the burning ghats that were consuming their late husbands). Abolishing *sut-tee*, Ms. Tonsich said sternly, "may be viewed as culturally dis-ruptive."

At best, the margin for these countries was very thin, and the prospects were poor. "The underdeveloped countries are not simply less prosperous models of the wealthy nations," an Afri-can professor said at his inaugural lecture at the University of Ghana in 1961. "There are embedded in their structure factors which make for inertia and even retrogression." Yielding to those factors was the path of least resistance for the govern-ments of the tropical countries, and they stumbled down it, sustained by immense governmental and private loans.

Not all the poor countries will be losers. Mexico and Brazil, Europe-oriented for centuries, are clearly en route to full-scale modernity, though prosperity will come to the Brazilian northeast as slowly as it came to the American South. Thailand, Malaysia, and Singapore seem to have been able to respond quickly enough to price/cost signals to make their futures hopeful (Thailand had never grown corn until the Japanese developed feedlots for beef and demanded it, and today southern Thailand is full of corn); oil gives Nigeria and Venezuela at least a breather. The fact that Africa as a continent is still underpopulated means that the problems of its people must be manageable, but they clearly are not being managed.

The full irresponsibility of the leadership of the Third World was revealed in the whoop of joy with which they greeted the triumph of the oil cartel. No greater disaster could have befallen them, not only because the cost of energy in their own economies would rise but also because the modern nations, being forced to pay more for oil, would be able to pay less for what the poor countries had to export. It is hard to feel sorry for people whose hatreds lie so near the surface and can so easily defeat even their self-interest; but the dimensions of the tragedy ahead of them are infinitely pitiable.

Cristo é fermato a Eboli, the Calabrian peasants told Carlo Levi, but for better or worse they do get the chance to go north, beyond Eboli. In the poor countries humanity numbered over a billion souls is trapped and hopeless, waiting for famine and pestilence. There is, I suppose, one possible technological fix: the development of genetic biology to the point where mothers can choose the sex of the fetus. This sort of genetic manipulation is already within the reach of biological researchers; its specter is one of the major reasons why they are now meeting in special congresses and proposing agreements to limit each other's explorations.

Choice of sex in the poor countries (probably in the rich countries, too) would be overwhelmingly for a male child, and as the reproduction of the race depends upon the numbers of female children population growth would quickly slam to a halt. "Not only would the population explosion cease to be a danger," Marion Levy argues, "but the extinction of humankind might become a lively possibility." There never has been a human society in which men outnumbered women in the ratios Levy believes would occur (as high as ten to one in some cultures); free choice of the sex of offspring would break the bonds of preexisting culture much more completely than wall posters denoucing Confucius and reeducation sessions. What culture would then emerge, nobody can predict; but one does not have to be a feminist to regard the prospect with fear and loathing.

It is nonsense to say that very poor and very rich societies cannot coexist in peace; they always have and they do, and the tensions that make the world uncomfortable today have little to do with income differentials. For the people who live in the modernized societies, the blow ahead will be to their self-image, as they come to accept the idea that on this rich and fecund earth members of their species are dying like insects. It is our fault, too: with what seemed to us and indeed was a purity of goodwill, we gave the tropical poor the tools for their own destruction. These tools they accepted; the others in the kit they turned down, encouraged in that suicidal folly by renegades from western cultures, who did not understand, did not care to understand, the interrelationships of their own societies. The *trahison des clercs* of our time has been a nuisance and an occasionally sickening entertainment in the rich countries the clerks seek to betray; it has made catastrophe all but inevitable for the tropical poor.

7

Governance and Reality: The Statistical Focus

*The instantaneous origination of obvious expedients is of
no use when the field is already covered with the
heterogeneous growth of complex past expedients;
bit-by-bit development is out of place unless you are
sure which bit should and which bit should not be
developed; the extension of customs may easily mislead
when there are so many customs; no immense and
involved subject can be set right except by faculties
which can grasp what is immense and scrutinise what is
involved. But mere common sense is here matched with
more than it can comprehend, like a schoolboy in the
differential calculus—and absorption in the present
difficulty is an evil, not a good, for what is wanted is
that you should be able to see many things at once, and
take in their bearings, not fasten yourself on one thing.
The characteristic danger of great nations, like the
Romans or the English, which have a long history of
continuous creation, is that they may at last fail from
not comprehending the great institutions which they
have created.*

—*Walter Bagehot (1876)*

1

Affluence, technology, demographic waves—all change, all to
some degree increase, the functions of governance.

First, a productive society relies on government, more than
its members realize, for the promotion of the complex relationships subsumed under the rubric interdependence. From early

on, the markets formed in the shadow of the castle, for protection; and the Roman roads were bent to bring them through the market square. (Drivers in England and France to this day can curse such "city planning.") With each generation, the promotion of commerce has become more detailed and complicated: money coinage, weights and measures, postal services, patent and copyright, rivers and harbors, canal construction, land grants for railroad builders, airports and air traffic control, the interstate highway system, wire transfer of funds by the Federal Reserve. The court system itself grew up primarily (not, of course, exclusively) as a device for the resolution of commercial disputes with minimal disruption of ongoing business.

But commerce had to be regulated as well as promoted. In the Middle Ages, such rules were promulgated in large part by consensus: the establishment and inspection of standard weights, the location and timing of markets. Then the special interests of the state began to find expression: to place the new centers of wealth and influence under government control, and to make them sources of financial gain to government, monopolies of export and import and the production of staple commodities were sold for the benefit of the state treasury, and subsequently protected by state power. (We study these monopolies as quaint stories from the reign of Queen Elizabeth I, but they existed in the United States, too, until the effort by its proprietor to keep his toll bridge the sole bridge over the Charles River between Boston and Cambridge provoked the Supreme Court of 1837 to a sudden burst of common sense.) Presently the state was regulating in a proclaimed public interest, controlling the prices of the natural monopolies (grain elevators, railroads, telephone companies, electric utilities) and restrictively licensing enterprises that would destroy each other if left to free competition (banks chartered to one place; broadcasting "stations," a very pure example, chartered of technical necessity to a single frequency band).

As interdependence increases, "policy" questions arise. Procedures are laid down for preventing collusion, for financing enterprise, for collective bargaining between employers and employees. Where enterprise requires extremely complicated technological service or special legal treatment, government acquires a directing role—the construction of dams with their power-generating and irrigating capacities; atomic energy; the placement of natural gas pipelines. Finally, the wheel comes full circle, and government returns to an ever more complicated establishment of legal weights and measures—agricultural grading, product safety and even (in the drug field) product efficacy, automotive efficiencies, etc. Law establishes Milton Katz's "legal order" to allocate the costs of different activities among different beneficiaries and victims. Ultimately, the government's role in the *promotion* of economic activity is very nearly forgotten—may even, indeed, seem suspect. This, too, has happened before: "By a stroke of bad luck," Raymond de Roover noted sourly in his analysis of the troubles of Florence and of the Medici family in the fifteenth century, "Cosimo was survived by Piero, the elder of his two legitimate sons, who had been reared to rule but received no training in the counting house." Prosperity breeds heedlessness of the productivity that created it, and fury at anyone who suggests that you must keep the goose in good health if you want the golden eggs.

As a side effect of the increasing mobility and division of labor, the caring functions once performed within the family are assigned to the state; affluence generates an ever growing welfare department. Public safety, always the first function of government, is extended from the domain of military defense and criminal justice to fire protection, water supply, waste disposal, health services. History's aged and infirm become today's senior citizens. In periods of dramatic demographic change, the state must make special provisions—for schools in the 1950s, nursing homes today and tomorrow—to handle "problems" that are far beyond the capabilities of individual families or voluntary communities within the society. Because the government directs resources to the creation of goods and services that almost everyone considers necessary but that would not otherwise be produced, there arises a belief that all production should be controlled and its results allocated by deliberate political process.

The most important of all the changes wrought in democratic governance by the growth of affluence and the improvement of technology is the increase in government's ability to collect taxes. Once upon a time, the state lived off the property of its ruler (augmented, when the king went on travels with his court, by the property of his major vassals, and by the booty of war); service was exacted, then taxes were farmed to local magnates, who could collect them at a profit; the coinage was clipped (this still happens, of course, when the government runs a deficit and produces inflation by printing money to pay its bills); tariffs were imposed (in the original constitutional scheme, the federal government was supposed to live *entirely* on tariff receipts); charters and monopolies and exemptions from tariffs were sold. Now, with the universal use of money, government need merely dip its spoon into the income stream. The questions of how and where—and how large a spoon—become central to the real influence of government on what happens in the society.

Technology increases the reach of government action, enabling the transmittal of official signals almost as quickly (though nowhere near so pervasively) as the market transmission of price/cost signals. Flocks of lawyers roost at both corporate headquarters and government offices to serve as the carrier pigeons of enlarged regulation; daily newsletters flutter down upon the country to inform businessmen and their specialist helpers of the most recent decisions by government agencies, courts, and legislatures. Systemically, technology tends to reduce the significance of local, small-scale governmental units and increase that of large-scale, national units—just as it tends to overwhelm ethnicity and regional culture. Great bureaucracies grow to pass on the orders from central authority. Totalitarianism becomes possible: Solzhenitsyn is merely the most talented of those who have described what it can mean when a tyrant's mumbled wish that someone rid him of some meddling priest can be overheard by tens of thousands.

The horror of totalitarian government is the continual presence of that authority: nobody who stopped for a cup of coffee in the huge Café Moskva on Stalinallee in East Berlin in the 1950s or 1960s will ever forget the eerie experience of hearing so many spoons clatter against so many cups and saucers, because the normal masking sound of conversation was hushed by the customers' fear of who might be listening. But unless totalitarian procedures are adopted, the actual force of government action tends to be considerably less—and its vector considerably less predictable—than policy-makers believe. People continue to want things other than what the government has decided they want, producers fail to make what government has decided they should make, human energy and societal wealth leak off to counterstructures of disorganization half-consciously committed against the state. The bureaucracies are never large enough to accomplish their mission.

Bagehot stated the dilemma more than a hundred years ago: "A free intellectual community is a complicated network of ramified relations, interlacing and passing hither and thither, old and new,—some of fine city weaving, others of gross agricultural construction. You are never sure what effects any force or change may produce on a frame-work so exquisite and so involved. Govern as you may, it will be a work of great difficulty, labor, and responsibility; and no man who is thus occupied ought ever to go to bed without reflecting, that from the difficulty of his employment he may, probably enough, have that day done more harm than good." All the complexities have multiplied in the century since; but, unfortunately, the people thus occupied only rarely feel the force of Bagehot's "ought."

2

To date, we have had only small doses of troubles from the immodesties of leadership, because the American form of government has been wondrously flexible. The real bicentennial that should be celebrated will come in 1987, when the Constitution is two hundred years old. The purpose to be achieved by the organization is simply stated in the preamble: "to form a more perfect union, establish justice, insure domestic tranquillity, provide for the common defense, promote the general welfare, and secure the blessings of liberty to ourselves and our posterity."

Every schoolchild knows that the model on which the Founding Fathers worked was Montesquieu's three-legged stool, with government to rest equally on executive, legislative, and judicial branches. But I think that if one reads the document straight, without considering possible sources or later overlays, the Constitution intended congressional supremacy. The House of Representatives was to be the only body directly elected by the people (the Senate would be elected indirectly through state legislatures, the president indirectly through a sort of Court of Notables, men like the men meeting in Philadelphia to write the Constitution, in an Electoral College). For this reason, the House would hold the purse strings: taxes and appropriations could originate only in the House. And it was in taxes and appropriations, as the veterans of "No Taxation Without Representation!" knew well, that the essence of government resided.

Once the system had shaken down, the Congress was indeed the dominant body—except in foreign affairs, where presidents took the lead (Monroe, who once asserted his independent political position in a book denouncing Washington's failure to involve Congress in foreign policy, later proclaimed his Doctrine without even talking to any senator). But in the period between Madison and Lincoln—forty-four years—only Jackson's name rings as loud as the names of Webster, Clay, and Calhoun, all basically men of the Congress though they all served also in the vice-presidency or in cabinet posts. Much the same can be said for the period between Lincoln and Theodore Roosevelt, when Blaine, Sherman, Conkling, Tom Reed, and Bryan were all more important as policy-makers than anyone elected to the presidency except Cleveland—and all but Reed served at one time or another in some part of the executive office. (Let me note in passing that the idea of executive and legislative branches entirely separate in personnel, with almost no members of either having had experience in the other, would have seemed ludicrous to the Founding Fathers and to the nineteenth century; it was an unintended secondary consequence of the ironclad seniority system imposed on the House in the early twentieth century by a reform movement seeking to break the power of the Speaker.)

But the increasing unification of the country, brought about by the railroads and early telecommunications, was destroying the old balance between the states and the federal government, and imposing upon the national government tasks that the framers of the Constitution could not have imagined. Theodore Roosevelt made the presidency a bully pulpit; and war gave Woodrow Wilson, like Lincoln before him, the chance to convert the authority of the president to the authority of a commander-in-chief. In the end, congressional resistance reduced and destroyed Wilson, as it had Lincoln's successor; but governmentally a new world had indeed been born. As Felix Frankfurter wrote in the 1920s, "The 'great society,' with its permeating influence of technology, large-scale industry, and progressive urbanization, presses its problems." It was Wilson's successor, the ineffectual Warren Harding, apparently under the thumb of the Congress whence he had come, who changed the balance of American government by creating a national budgeting function independent of the Congress.

Since the administration of John Adams there had been no executive budget in the government of the United States. Each department of the federal government drew up its own funding requests and submitted them directly to Congress, which appropriated funds for narrowly specified purposes. The president could not amend the departmental requests before they were sent to Congress (indeed, he often found out about them when Congress received them), and neither he nor the department heads had legal power to transfer funds from one purpose to another (though of course they did it anyway). As a last knotting of the rope, Congress never appropriated enough money to keep a department going for a full year, and before the year ended virtually every department of government was back before its masters, begging for money. It was by no means unknown for departments of the United States government to borrow money from private sources to meet their payrolls.

The power of the modern presidency starts with the Budget and Accounting Act of 1921. Because the Bureau of the Budget was to be a subordinate part of the Treasury Department, and to work entirely as a service agency for the president, Congress did not retain the power to approve the nomination of its director; and when Franklin Roosevelt moved the Bureau to his new Executive Office in 1939 Congress treated the matter as a minor reorganization. Not until 1973 did the Congress demand the power to confirm or deny a president's appointment of a director for what was now, after a Nixon initiative, a much-expanded Office of Management and Budget. But as Lewis Dexter once said, the federal budget is "the work plan of the nation." Programs are meaningless without funding, and law can be enforced only if resources are allocated for the purpose. If the budget provides tea tasters to work in the customs office in the Port of New Orleans but only a handful of examiners across the country to look into occupational safety conditions, then tea grading will be expertly done but legislation and court orders written to assure safe working conditions are likely to be nothing more than exercises in draftsmanship.

Beginning with the budget for fiscal 1977, Congress will try to exercise a more general oversight, and everything will be pushed off a few months (the fiscal year will run October through September rather than July through June); but the basic process will continue essentially as it has been. The president will present, as before, a unified document that has been hammered out in negotiations with the departments, mostly via the Office of Management and Budget. Then each branch of

Congress separately will undertake a two-step process that is peculiarly (in more ways than one) American.

First comes an examination of the desirability of the program to be funded, which is carried on by committees and subcommittees specialized in the subject area—defense, education and labor, commerce, etc. This produces an "authorization" without which money cannot be spent by the executive branch. Before World War II, the authorization was general, but it became increasingly clear that the magnitude of the money was a major factor in the effectiveness of a program, and the authorization process began to include numbers. Since the 1950s, members of the substantive subcommittees have had a chance to be heroes for proponents of programs, who could campaign for "full funding" and dream of very large sums coming their way when the new fiscal year began.

Employees of the executive departments are formally bound by the verdict of the Office of Management and Budget; though they may admit that they asked for more than they got, they are required to tell the congressional committees that their jobs can be done for the figures printed in the president's budget. What they say to members of the committees off the record, of course, cannot be policed. During the authorization process, the budget invariably grows. One of the large purposes of the reforms that go into effect with the 1977 budget is to discipline the authorizing committees.

Authorization goes to the president and is duly signed. Then the question of how much money shall *really* be spent on this program goes to the relevant subcommittee of the House Appropriations Committee. It has often been observed that free-spending liberals levitate toward the committees that authorize, while tight-fisted conservatives gravitate into the committees that appropriate. What happens in the appropriations subcommittee is the stuff of government, where the interests of the constituents the congressman represents merge with the intensity of his own feelings to create trading positions, and committee chairmen perform both leadership and mediating functions. The heart of popular representation in the American governmental process lies in the meetings of the House Appropriations subcommittees, which are permanent and exclusive (that is, their members hold no other committee assignments); and future historians may find that the worst thing that happened to American government in 1973, which is saying a good deal, was the decision to open these meetings for public inspection. Negotiation requires that men show a willingness to abandon previous positions before they are precisely certain of the quid pro quo, and no one performing a representative function can ever do that in public. To date, having won the battle to open the subcommittee meetings, the reformers have made no use of the new arrangements; but if the unified budget begins to pinch, fanatics for particular programs will have a weapon to sabotage the appropriations process.

From the House subcommittees, the appropriations measures pass to the full House committee, thence to the floor of the House, thence to a subcommittee of the Senate, which serves essentially as a court of appeals against cuts taken in the lower house; and then to the full Senate committee, and then to the floor of the Senate, and then to a joint committee that reconciles the differences . . . With statistics arriving weekly from the Federal Reserve Board and monthly from the departments of Labor and Commerce—and the most recent piece of awful news showing up all but immediately on the television screens —it is not surprising that people grow cynical about the capacity of the Congress to govern.

Budgeting and taxing are the central activities of any serious legislative body; it is the "money bills," and only the money bills, that actually must be passed every year; everything else is optional. Intellectually, however, this labor is relatively easy, because the final bills are necessarily "incremental": the committees start with an existing budget "line" or an existing tax schedule, and decide whether to augment or diminish it. And for this purpose, obviously, the testimony of the people who are already living with the budget or processing the tax returns must be crucial, because they know so much more than anybody else.

Establishing new programs and writing new rules of the road —for political campaigning, fuel conservation, job safety, environmental protection, equal rights, pension plan qualification— are obviously much more difficult tasks, and normally take years to accomplish. The basic tool employed is the committee hearing, in which the people who would be affected by the new legislation (and advocates of various kinds, paid or unpaid) appear to plead their causes. Specific questions can be referred for neutral answer to the committees' own staffs, the Congressional Reference Service of the Library of Congress, or occasionally the General Accounting Office, a highly professionalized service of the Congress that can express opinions as well as audit books, of private as well as public organizations. And when the bills are to be written, each branch of Congress has its own specialized legislative drafting staff (the House staff is especially well regarded). Bills can be introduced, of course, only by members of Congress, not by representatives of the executive.

Still, the fact of the matter is that the basic legislative program on which the Congress works is now set in motion, almost as completely as the budgetary program, by the executive branch. The congressional staffs are mostly high in quality, but much smaller than would be necessary to analyze all the information that comes flooding to their desks. Thus the needs to be met by legislation tend to be defined by the much larger executive departments and the more specialized regulatory agency staffs; and the projections of what any section of any bill means must be made within the executive branch.

An old law from 1919, still on the books, forbids members of the executive branch to "lobby" for legislation, which is pretty funny. In fact, every department of the executive branch has its own permanent "congressional liaison" staff. Under the Kennedy and Johnson administrations, the White House took direct command of these staffs; Lyndon Johnson said on several occasions that next to the cabinet officer himself, the chief of the congressional liaison staff was the most important man in the department. It should also be noted that there is no such thing as a congressman who does not occasionally need a favor for a constituent from the executive branch, and also that the executive departments have direct access to citizens' groups in their clientele, whose disaffection could be a nuisance to a congressman in the next campaign.

Failure of a bill to clear a committee will doom it, but a bill, like an authorization, may be reported favorably by a committee without any serious purpose to make the thing real, as a means of propitiating an individual or a group. Recently, with the Congress and the presidency in the hands of different political parties, the temptations to irresponsibility have grown, because the president can propose with absolute certainty that nothing will happen and the Congress can pass bills the president has promised to veto, each gaining credit with constituents at no cost to the country.

3

The system has one great advantage: it is, for all the occasional interference of tyrannical chairmen, profoundly democratic. Congressmen do feel, very deeply, that they represent the people of their districts. Because the real work is done in committees, the individual congressman is constantly in situations where his vote—which he correctly translates as the vote of his district—will count. In legislative assemblies where everything important happens on the floor, the individual representative is a cipher. Being a Member of Congress is orders of magnitude more important than being a Member of Parliament, because Congress works in committees. There is no monolithic majority that can be controlled by party office or even by a president; instead, action is taken by shifting ad hoc majorities. In the logrolling process, intensities of feeling have weight. This surely is the essence of democracy, and of the doctrine of the importance of the individual—that intensities as well as mere numbers count in the decision-making process. Yet the sad fact is that generations of American children and newspaper readers have been brought up to believe that logrolling is the bane rather than the glory of the legislative system, and that some system resting on public plebiscite would be a "more perfect" democracy rather than a model of authoritarian government. Theodore Lowi correctly sees "participation for its own sake" as "greasing the skids toward popularly based tyranny." Most of the "reforms" proposed to make Congress "more responsive" would severely damage its democratic nature.

Another major advantage of the existing system is the opportunity congressmen have to learn from experience, and to learn the personal characteristics both of their colleagues and of the members of the executive branch who repeatedly come before them. Relatively permanent committee assignments give congressmen an expertise in a limited subject matter which is simply indispensable if intelligent decisions are to be made. (This is often criticized because of the tendency for the knowledgeable to favor "special interests" at the expense of a presumably broader "public interest," a tendency seen by one group of critics as an unconscionable advantage for an industry regulated by law, by another group of critics as a dangerous willingness to raid the Treasury on behalf of the policies of a government department with which the members of the committee have long-standing and cozy relationships. But the bias that the world's work must be done is nearly inescapable under any system of organization, and surely more sound than what the critics seem to want, which is total suspicion of any organization, public or private, which does in fact get something done.) Even more important is the chance to learn which of the many people who come before a committee, and which of one's colleagues in the small group, will have valuable contributions to make.

It has long been fashionable to make fun of J. P. Morgan's comment that he lent money to people only on the basis of his judgment of their character, but the fact is that personal trust and respect are the normal basis for most private and important public decisions. The smoke-filled room is usually a better place than the convention floor for the choice of a presidential nominee—and the attitude of the professional Democratic reformers, that such decisions should really be made by people who do not personally know the candidates, is unspeakable idiocy in both theory and practice. The real case for decentralization of governmental functions is not that people on the scene know the situation, but that they know each other.

At the end of a remarkably successful career in the Department of State, the Bureau of the Budget, and the National Aeronautics and Space Administration, James E. Webb said, "In any governmental position, you've got somehow to find a way to create a basis of confidence on which you can build effective relationships. . . . A lot of what it takes is just human confidence and trust." Then, he added, one could hope to achieve "Mary Parker Follett's idea of a synthesis upward to the highest common factor instead of a compromise downward, as a fundamental of group action." The congressional committee system, for all its advertised problems, is a system reasonably well suited to achieve Webb's conditions and Mrs. Follett's hopes. To the extent that the committees themselves win trust and respect from the House or Senate as a whole, the benefits are gained on the largest scale. Of course it doesn't always work right; what does?

But the disadvantages of the current legislative machinery are very grave, and increasingly dangerous at a time when affluence, interdependence, and technological leverage make government decision more frequent, more pervasive, and more long-lasting than ever before. The most obvious of them is the bias toward negativism in the system as a whole—action can be stopped at any stage from the initial subcommittee consideration to the meeting of the joint committee of the two houses that is supposed to reconcile disparate versions of a bill both have passed. In the minds of the authors of the Constitution, the Congress was to be the initiating body, with the president given a veto power to restrain it. In the decision-making process operating today, the presidency is the initiating body, and the veto power lies with Congress—even, on occasion, a handful of congressmen. The publicized confrontation between the 94th Congress and President Ford is not in fact an exception to this rule, because most of the legislation that was vetoed had been built on the chassis of executive recommendations; what provoked most of the vetoes was congressional amendment, not congressional initiative.

A further bias toward negativism is inescapable in publicized politics, because every change in policy yields costs as well as benefits, and the costs are almost never just financial. People are much more certain to vote against something that has harmed or frightened them than they are to vote for something that has helped them. The voter asks, "What have you done for me lately?"; he remembers unaided anything you did *to* him twelve years ago. It is one thing for a congressman to argue in committee session behind closed doors that a given benefit is worth a given cost, and something else entirely for him to stand naked before those who are paying the cost, admitting that he knew of their troubles and voted for the bill anyway.

But the worst failure of the Congress, in the context of these pages, has been in the exercise of its positive, law-writing function, where too often the committees have shown incapacity or unconcern in predicting the impact of legislation on the real world. We have noted the Clean Air Act and ethnicity, the waste of resources on rail transit, the tax breaks given to feedlot operators. The worst examples are the subsidies given without thought to what the private market will in fact do with the money when it arrives, and in this category the overwhelming failure is the Medicare law, with its Medicaid "sleeper" provisions, the costs of which are now running something over $15 billion a year, more than half of which simply pours into the pockets of the nation's doctors and hospital and nursing home personnel without improving medical care for anyone. Meanwhile, medical service becomes increasingly hard to find both in rural areas and on the streets of the urban slums, and an entirely disproportionate share of medical attention goes to the chronic, hopeless ills of the aged at the expense of children and young adults whose needs would be a much wiser investment of the resources. The national health insurance bills now pending in Congress will not remedy this situation and may well make it worse; some of the most distinguished proponents of Senator Kennedy's proposal (Rashi Fein of the Harvard Medical School, for example) have even taken the position that the bill should be supported *because* it will produce a complete breakdown in the current system of delivery of health services in the United States.

What happens in these situations is that government looks to something that is going wrong here and now, and seeks to remedy that; and the political pressures are for the simplest and quickest available means (i.e., if food prices are going up, clamp a ceiling on food prices). At the hearings in committee, more or less expert witnesses from government, academia, or industry may question the effects of proposed legislation, but all futures are soft, and the hard testimony, which commands the most congressional and press attention, tends to be reportorial, specifics of existing woes. Medicare legislation sought to remedy a condition in which the people with the most diseases, the aged, had the least resources to pay the costs of medical help; the Medicaid kicker, which was added on the floor without committee hearings, made similar federal help available to those states which would establish and partially finance programs to provide medical services to the nonaged poor and near-poor. This financing was done, incidentally, outside the appropriations process; Congress committed the federal government to put up three dollars for every one dollar state governments could find for such programs. Eventually, of course, it became necessary to impose a dollar limit on federal assistance to any one state.

The legislation relied upon the market mechanism to reallocate existing resources, and sought to prevent price increases by forbidding payments greater than the fees doctors or hospitals charged patients who paid their own bills. It was apparently not understood that both doctors and hospitals were being put in a position where they could profitably raise all their charges, because any reduction in the numbers of private paying patients would be more than made up by an inflow of new customers financed by the government. Because neither the new federal programs nor the established Blue Cross and Blue Shield insurance programs controlled costs or prices, neither doctors nor hospitals were under the slightest pressure to operate economically. The higher their costs, the higher their prices, and the more they got from the government and the insurance companies. From 1965 to 1968, the nation's total expenditure for medical care rose 40 percent—from $35 billion to $50 billion—with relatively little increase in the total care delivered.

Before the Medicare and Medicaid legislation, doctors in the biggest cities had on the average earned less than doctors in small towns and rural areas; the market supplied economic incentives to live away from the metropolitan centers, which would otherwise be most appealing. Once the government started to pick up the bills, this income differential diminished; and in the United States, as in the underdeveloped countries, medical talent drifted to the cities.

(It should be noted, however, that in 1975 a stroke of luck slowed the drift. Deprived of some of their automobile accident income by no-fault insurance, personal-injury lawyers had turned their attention to cases involving possible negligence by doctors, with predictable inflation of medical malpractice insurance rates. County-seat juries know their doctors and are likely to be sympathetic rather than angry at a doctor's bad luck; insurance rates are therefore lower for rural practice, creating a powerful new incentive for the country doctor to stay where he is and for the newly licensed doctor to accept life in the sticks.)

Within the cities, doctors whose practices centered in hospitals (excepting surgeons) had on the average earned less than doctors who maintained private offices outside. Now this differential, too, eroded—with extreme consequences. Nobody in or out of the profession seems to have realized how much happier doctors are when they can work in hospitals, where they receive a very high degree of deference from the staffs, devote the greatest proportion of their time to economically productive activity, and—most important of all—participate constantly in the collegial relationships that constitute a good share of the psychic income of any profession. Increasingly, doctors assigned to hospitals, even for minor treatment, patients whose bills were to be paid by the government. The costs of the medical programs shot up—but even more important, doctors in ever-increasing numbers abandoned neighborhood practice. The day of the house call had long since darkened; now the day of the convenient office entered a twilight. Surgeons and operations proliferated, because the government would pay for surgery. By no means all the operations were medically necessary.

What we have now, in short, is a program so expensive that the costs average out to almost 2 percent of the income of each American family—and so poorly planned that the number of people whose medical care has been improved is considerably smaller than the number of people whose medical care has been diminished. And nearly everything that has gone wrong with it was predictable.

Again: the Kennedy and Johnson administrations were dismayed by the deterioration of the housing stock in the center cities. A program was designed and funded to give subsidies and tax credits to builders, renovators, and lenders willing to work in the slums, and to insure them against losses from the special risks of operating in marginal and depressed neighborhoods. It was generally agreed both in the executive branch and in Congress that this insurance would never have to be paid, because the builders and banks were wrong in their estimate of the degree of risk involved. There was no fail-safe provision for government if the private business view turned out to be correct; worse yet, there was no consideration given to the likelihood that the combination of quick tax-free profits and guarantees against losses would draw into work in slum housing a quasi-criminal element that would impartially (often legally) defraud both the purchasers of their work and the government. The result was not only that the United States became through foreclosure proceedings the biggest slumlord in history, but also that the limited resources available for real improvement were squandered in ways that hastened the decay of the cities. Because of this program and its administration, Chicago's Mayor Daley told a Senate hearing in mid-1975, "most major cities in the United States have been left with thousands of abandoned and vandalized structures in what had been desirable neighborhoods."

Other aspects of the housing program were equally ruinous. Because the subsidy offered applied to the mortgage, the government was committed to keep paying for the life of the mortgage, in most cases thirty years; every year, funds that might have been available to help build new housing were already committed to continuing subsidy for old houses. (Allowed to run its full ten years, which it was not, the program enacted in 1968 would have left the government spending $7.5 billion a year for the twenty years after 1978, simply to sustain what had already been done.) Because the subsidy was related to the purchaser's or tenant's income, the government's outlays rose as the cost of the housing rose, stimulating builders to provide the most the law allowed and occupants to undertake more than they could afford. (Central air conditioning may seem an unnecessary luxury if you have to pay the full cost yourself, but if the government will pay half . . .) As Pat Moynihan observed about the poverty program in his book *Maximum Feasible Misunderstanding,* "This is the essential fact: *the government did not know what it was doing."*

What is especially disheartening about such stories is that Congress should be the branch of government that looks ahead. Its committees are led by veterans who have been living with the subject of their deliberations for some years, and whose reelection is pretty well guaranteed. Between the Congressional Reference Service and the committee staffs, there is no reason why they should not receive thorough briefings; the departments in the executive office, academic experts, and all those affected by a proposed program are more than willing to contribute input to the hearing process. Whatever the faults of the committee process in decision-making, it is undoubtedly the best way to gather a variety of predictions of the future impact of proposed changes, as seen from different perspectives.

Moreover, the committeeman's expertise is an overlay—while his work on this committee may be the most important thing he does in the Congress, his mailbox back at the office is stuffed with constituents' concerns about other matters. He retains his sense of the opportunity costs incurred by the allocation of resources to this rather than that program, he cannot afford to be a fanatic, he need never abandon his common sense. Too often, alas, he does.

During the Kennedy and Johnson administrations, I sat on something called the President's Panel on Educational Research and Development, and to our monthly meeting one day came a pair of young sociologists who had designed what later became the Job Corps, an outstanding disaster of the poverty program. Among the members of the panel was a lean Virginian named Ralph Flynt, an Associate Commissioner of Education nearing retirement. He listened carefully to the young sociologists' analysis of the pathologies of the ghetto, until finally he said, "Look. You're going to take these kids out of Harlem and put them in full-time training programs in Missoula, Montana. How are you going to get them there?"

"I guess we'll give them plane tickets," said one of the young sociologists rather airily.

"You'd better have a budget for people to find them again after you give them the plane tickets," said Ralph Flynt. "What are you going to do about the urine?"

The sociologists were struck dumb.

"I can assure you," said Ralph Flynt, "they'll make water

three times a day, maybe more. Who's designing the bath-
rooms, and the sewage system? Who's going to run the camp?"

None of these questions, or the dozen like them that followed, had been in the purview of the sociologists. They had
two visions—one of miserable and incompetent teen-agers de-
parting from city streets, the other of self-respecting and capable young adults returning to those streets—and to get from one
to the other they had an idea, for which they wanted (and got)
money. The *details,* they finally said scornfully when they
recovered their aplomb, were less important than the concep-
tion.

Flynt had a practical suggestion for them. In the mid-1960s,
tens of thousands of army noncoms were reaching retirement
age and were available at quite reasonable wages to work in
camps. They were experienced at handling the sort of problem
the Job Corps entrants would provide: the army of World War
II had taught more illiterates to read than all the adult education programs before or since. The young sociologists should
solicit advice from the army, and should recruit a cadre of
retiring noncoms, design a program with their cooperation, and
only then seek funding . . .

Well! You could see the shock and outrage barely repressed
in our academic visitors. The congressmen to whom they were
selling the program weren't talking to them like that. But, of
course, the congressmen should have been talking like that.

During the hearings on what became the Pension Reform Act
of 1974, one of the expert witnesses complained that this was
the third year the House subcommittee had held such meetings, and there still wasn't a law ready to be proposed. Subcommittee chairman John H. Dent said he was glad to be holding
a third year of hearings—if he'd had to write a law after the first
or second year, he now realized, he'd have written a bad one:
this was a more complicated subject than his expert seemed to
realize. Dent is one of those heartening American phenomena:
in appearance, a mustache-Pete; in manner, a pompous blow-
hard; in fact, an able and conscientious legislator—there are

more congressmen like that than you think, or than our self-important press would have you believe. He was looking ahead, to the impact of his legislation; the expert was looking back, at the evils he wished to expunge.

Generals, it is said, are always prepared to fight the last war. Congressmen too often write remedies for last year's wrongs, egged on by people who should, but don't, know better. Something more intellectually ambitious will be required of our legislators if we are to avoid stagnation or worse in the last quarter of this century. It is precisely the task of establishing the parameters of projection that cannot be left to the experts.

4

But much else must be left to experts, for government intervention in the affairs of a complicated society involves too many little laws—definitions, rules, incentives, penalties, exceptions, inclusions, adaptations—for any general legislative body to master the needs. Nor can decentralization to state and local government help, for the state and local legislatures are technologically even more limited than Congress. Much of what really matters in government has to be left in the hands of bureaucrats, because nobody else will ever find the time to do it.

This need for bureaucracies equipped to exercise discretion gives rise to formal problems of great gravity in the American (and the English) system of government. One of the great traditions of the common law, fortunately not specifically written into the Constitution, forbade the legislature to delegate its rule-making authority to the executive. The solution was the regulatory commission, which constitutionally forms an arm of Congress, not a part of the executive branch. This is damned awkward, because the SEC, FCC, FTC, FPC, ICC, CAB, NLRB, and AEC (now NRC) have always spent less time on their rule-making activities than they do on executive and quasi-judicial functions. People *think* of the alphabet agencies and the Federal Reserve Board as part of the executive rather than part of the legislature. The president appoints their commissioners and governors, with the consent of the Senate, and in 1926 the Supreme Court ruled that he could also remove them at his pleasure, as he could remove cabinet officers. In 1935, having observed the use made of such powers by Coolidge and Roosevelt, the Court changed its mind and ruled that the commissioners of the regulatory agencies were entitled to serve out their legal term whether the president liked them or not.

Even more peculiar than these independent agencies are the many very similar bodies—EPA, OHSA, FEA, CPSA, LEAA (to mention only those of recent formation)—housed within the traditional executive departments but reporting directly to Congress and exercising authority not merely to "execute" but also to write the laws. Between them, the independent and the executive regulatory bureaus form the central institution supporting our effort to adapt an eighteenth-century form of government to late-twentieth-century needs. They establish the rules of the road for virtually all economic activity. Their growing pains on occasion have had a true Booth Tarkington flavor —for example, the case where a corporation was protesting the imposition of a fine for some prohibited activity, which got all the way to the Supreme Court before it was discovered that the regulation allegedly violated had been amended out of existence in a rule change that had never been published anywhere. This case led to the founding of the Federal Register, unquestionably the nation's most important periodical, a daily almost as long as this book containing the texts of new rules and regulations fresh from the agency and executive bakeshops, legally binding on everybody.

Unfortunately, despite their extraordinary authority, the record of the agencies is disastrous. They are the worst victims of technological overload and the least legitimate of our decision-making mechanisms.

The Securities and Exchange Commission mismanaged the modernization of the securities industry, first failing to require a uniform computer procedure that would have enabled small houses to compete against technologically more sophisticated big houses, then mandating an all-out competition the little firm has to lose.

The Federal Communications Commission delayed for ten years the operation of the domestic communications satellite, insisting on a competence it could not possess, to establish all the parameters of ownership, capacity, and use for a technology that was still in its infancy.

The Federal Power Commission by setting the price of natural gas at a level far below the likely market price encouraged overconsumption of our cleanest fuel (including the continuing wastage of billions of cubic feet a year by pilot lights in gas stoves) and discouraged the search for new supplies.

The Interstate Commerce Commission by insisting on its authority to set every route and rate for every category of freight created preposterous diseconomies like trucks that cannot take the direct route to their destination and must return empty even if cargoes are available to be carried; and not even the energy crisis could bend these sacred rules.

The Food and Drug Administration has prohibited cyclamates, which are probably safe, and encouraged saccharines, which are probably dangerous; the Environmental Protection Administration has generated both inflation and unemployment in a single-minded pursuit of abstract and arbitrary "standards"; the Civil Aeronautics Board has forced Americans to pay more than they should pay for air travel while planes fly more than half empty and airlines go broke; and the Federal Trade Commission, "policing" advertising and competitive practice in the marketplace, serves the economy as a vermiform appendix that has no function but to become inflamed.

Businessmen, bankers, labor leaders, and congressmen agree that the Federal Reserve Board is primarily responsible for the major recession of 1975. I happen to think the Fed is more to be pitied than censured, but as the only person who seems to agree with me is its chairman Arthur Burns, we probably ought to throw that one in, too.

Yet it is upon the skills and forecasting abilities of these agencies that we must rest the quality of government intervention in our society in the last quarter of this century. Administrative law, precisely because it controls the details, exerts much more force on daily activities than legislated or judge-made law. Even in the criminal justice area, what really counts is the administrative discretion of the district attorney, exercised in large cities subject to office codes never publicly revealed. Nationally, much of this law ("affirmative action" and its assorted quotas, for example) is created by executive departments, especially Labor, HEW, HUD, Agriculture, Transportation, and (especially through its subsidiary Internal Revenue Service) the Treasury. Most is written by the agencies. In both the executive departments and the agencies, the process has been captured by legislatively minded temporary civil servants whose training is legal rather than technical—that is, administrative law has become goal-directed rather than experience-based. The question of what will actually *happen* when the new rules are applied has become peripheral rather than central in the writing of administrative regulation—but the Congress delegated its authority to the regulatory agencies and bureaus only because they were presumed to know more about the practical results of policies.

Reorganization of the administrative law sector of the control system will be the most important single task for Congress in the remainder of this decade. It is an extremely difficult task, partly because it requires the articulation of what Chief Justice Taft rather wickedly called "intelligible principles," partly because the agencies and the rule-making bureaus in the executive departments are inherently extra-constitutional: while necessary to provide the substance of modern government, they are outside the American form. Moreover, there is no political payoff for a congressman in becoming involved with the operations of the agencies: the line that separates delegating authority from ducking responsibility was crossed long ago. What pressure there is to make these agencies responsible comes from "public interest" groups who would rather work through the courts and the press because they distrust all democratic process. They win their cases, too, and it doesn't much matter; because we really do live in a democratic society. To make significant changes in the United States in the domain touched by government requires at least the assent of the elected representatives of the people. As it should; as, one hopes, it always will.

8

Governance and Reality: The Particular Focus

The drive for self-determination and participatory democracy conflicts with the need for central direction of an increasingly complex and interconnected social organism. The drive to protect and preserve the ecology of the planet is in conflict with the constantly rising material aspirations of ever larger segments of the world's population. The drive towards more egalitarian, less competitive, social relations seems to conflict with the need for a meritocracy capable of dealing effectively with the complexities of a technological civilization. The anti-intellectual, anti-knowledge, anti-expertise trend of opinion, which is related to but goes beyond the egalitarian drive, conflicts with the requirement of increasing rationality and subtlety for men to live together without destroying each other. Modern societies have scarcely begun to grapple with this set of new internal contradictions. . . . Each of the conflicting trends . . . is a product of the same technological changes which have generated both personal aspiration and social complexity. . . . We have had such conflicting tendencies in the past, but they have seldom spread so quickly to so many people, a fact which is itself a product of the modern communications technology. National policy will somehow have to find a way to contain and channel these conflicts and contradictions. . . . The problem of technological forecasting has shifted from technology itself to society and politics.

—*Harvey Brooks (1969)*

1

When they are working properly, the executive and legislative branches take care of the country as a whole, seeking to direct its future course in all those areas (primarily but not exclusively economic) where men act in groups. We already live, of course, as Leibniz pointed out, in the best of all possible worlds (everything in it, Bradley added, is a necessary evil); nevertheless, the notion of a government directed entirely to statistical concerns and future developments has long frightened political scientists as well as ordinary people. In Britain, this fear produced the court of equity, where judges were supposed to do justice to the individual whatever the law might say, and also the remarkable (accidentally accomplished) principle that the state should protect the copyright of printed material without prior approval of what it said, which made possible what we now call freedom of the press.

Neither the courts nor the press are primarily instruments of governance. Even in the criminal justice system, the court does not "enforce the law": it decides the case. Courts are established for purposes of conflict resolution, and the criminal case becomes an instance of a dispute between an individual and society—if it reaches a court at all (90 percent of all arrests by the police are cleared through administrative process, either by guilty pleas or decisions not to prosecute). The press very vigorously does not consider itself part of the governance structure, neurotically rejecting all suggestions that the words "informing" and "governing" form a set with a sizable juncture; but ever since Macaulay looked up to the journalists' gallery in the House of Commons and saw a "fourth estate," cliché has kept the unacknowledged reality before the public mind.

The courts and the press do not get on very well with each other, never have and never will—what the lawyers and judges have to sell, after all, is procedure, and the press couldn't care less about that. But they do share two fundamental characteristics in their capacity as branches of the governance system.

Both are strongly oriented toward individual events and individual participants in those events, drawing their general conclusions from particular incidents rather than from statistical representations. And both look backward toward what is already on, or can be placed on, the record: for better or worse (it cuts both ways), they judge principles by the applications as observed. Justice Holmes once noted in a letter that he had heard law described as "the government of the living by the dead"; and the newspaper is notoriously good for one day only (the broadcast news report, for less than that). At the best, both are intensely responsible to the reality of the present, but they are unavoidably irresponsible to the reality of the future. They see the eggs, not the omelet.

It cuts both ways . . . There are reasons why the courts and the press are for so many the heroes of modern governance, and the reasons transcend the specifics of Watergate. People who tell you what is actually happening today are considerably more reliable—more trustworthy—than people who tell you what is going to happen tomorrow. To the extent that the act of governance is the direction of the future—and at bottom, I fear, this is what it is—neither the courts nor the press can be permitted to impose the significant decisions. But at the same time they must have their say and they must be heard, too, or at each point when the future becomes the present it will bear little resemblance to what the future was supposed to be. Breaking the eggs is easy; making the omelet takes talent; somebody has to ask why these eggs are being broken.

2

The first Chief Justice of the United States resigned that post to become governor of New York: the Founding Fathers would have been amazed to learn of Harold Laski's conclusion, a sesquicentennial later, that in the American system of government "sovereignty" resided in the Supreme Court. That institution would be, Hamilton wrote, "the least dangerous branch," having "neither FORCE nor WILL, but merely judgment." The first time the Court seriously inconvenienced anybody important (when it found for a claimant against the State of Georgia after the state refused to appear for trial), the Constitution was amended to remove the source of jurisdiction. The authority of the Court to upset the decisions of state supreme courts was given to it by the Judiciary Act in 1789, and save for a few exceptions detailed by the Fourteenth Amendment could presumably be removed by a subsequent act; the power to invalidate Acts of Congress was established, Learned Hand once insisted, "as a *coup de main*" without constitutional warrant. The Constitution specifically awards appellate jurisdiction to the Supreme Court only "with such exceptions, and under such regulations, as the Congress shall make."

John Marshall created the doctrine of judicial review in a very tricky decision, in which he declared the Court powerless to issue writs to cabinet officers because the Constitution had not given it such power; and Marshall knew that to be so because his Court had exclusive authority to declare what the Constitution said. Jefferson won his case but lost his argument; infuriated by Marshall and his friends, he had one of the Justices impeached by the House and came close to getting him convicted in the Senate. It certainly would never have occurred to Jefferson that he had to do something just because the Supreme Court said so, and both Jackson and Lincoln simply brushed aside Supreme Court decisions with which they disagreed. Grant packed the Court—increased the number of judges—to get a majority willing to allow the constitutionality of greenbacks (prior to Grant's two appointments, the Court had tentatively decided to invalidate as "legal tender" all the paper money Lincoln had printed); Franklin Roosevelt tried and failed to pack the Court to preserve his New Deal from judicial activism. Among the central tenets of LaFollette progressivism was the recall of Supreme Court decisions by popular referendum.

Jefferson, Jackson, Lincoln, Grant, Roosevelt, and LaFollette were all angry at the Court because it wouldn't let them do things they felt should be done. At bottom, in its governance role, the authority of the court system is that of the nay-sayer. "I do not care who makes the law iv a nation," said Mr. Dooley, "if I can get out an injunction." Resting its decisions as much as possible on precedent, necessarily looking back to the facts of the case rather than forward to the impact of its decision, the Supreme Court before the 1950s traditionally impeded national progress by preventing the states or Congress from legislating in areas where legislation was necessary. "In no major social or economic policy," Justice Robert H. Jackson, previously Franklin Roosevelt's attorney general, wrote sourly shortly before his death, "has time vindicated the Court."

But Jackson was about to participate (somewhat reluctantly) in a decision that would change the role of the Supreme Court in American society: *Brown* v. *Board of Education,* the end of "separate but equal." In form, the decision was traditional: it forbade school districts to assign children to schools other than their neighborhood schools, for purposes of racial segregation. In substance, by rejecting not some new piece of legislation but a long-standing and previously validated law, the decision obviously broke new ground. Because the Court was prohibiting something that was normal operating procedure in a large number of localities, it was consciously forcing governmental bodies to construct remedies for what was now established as their own malfeasance. The trial courts were ordered to supervise the construction process.

Alone among the governing institutions in America, the lower courts *must* decide. The litigants are in the courtroom; they say they demand justice, and they really do demand a resolution of their dispute. The trial judges—handling among them, of course, thousands of times as many cases as the Supreme Court ever sees—cannot duck the issues personalized in their courtrooms (a California law forbids the payment of a judge's salary if he has not reached his decision within ninety days of the completion of the case). The Supreme Court, however, can duck a decision, and often does, refusing to hear an appeal or deciding it on the narrowest possible grounds.

The lawyer's shibboleth says that "hard cases make bad law" —that in their desire to do justice between the parties, judges often establish precedents that will lead to worse injustices when other parties differently situated come to court to resolve their disputes. But it is at least as accurate to say that "bad law makes hard cases," that the judges find themselves unable to follow precedent or legislated law because the results in the cases before them seem inexcusably unfair. Henry Hart and Albert Sacks of the Harvard Law School once argued that malfunctions in the society necessarily show up first as court cases, because people have an absolute right to take their grievances to court, while they can bring their troubles to the legislature only through a gesture of grace by an elected representative. Thus, "Legislatures and administrative agencies tend always to make law . . . by alteration of the solutions first laid down by the courts."

Before *Brown*, few judges would have accepted the validity of the Hart and Sacks reasoning: their business, they would have said, was simply to declare what the law (or the Constitution) *is*, and at that Rubicon they had to wait. Since *Brown*, it has become commonplace for the Supreme Court to speak for the purpose of putting pressure on the legislature. Deciding a case involving cable television in a way that was manifestly unfair to broadcasters and program producers, for example, Justice Potter Stewart noted sarcastically, "We take the Copyright Act of 1909 as we find it"—and, obviously, there isn't anything about cable television in the Copyright Act of 1909.

Nearly a decade after that decision, Congress has still been unable to write a new Copyright Act that would cover cable television. In an age when changes in technology dictate changes in social organization, only the courts—technologically illiterate, wholly unable to measure the possible effects of what they say—have been willing to make the changes in the "legal order" that reflect or frustrate technological development. This nexus of congressional and executive immobility was what Earl Warren found in 1954, when he became the first Chief Justice to arrive on the bench directly from a governor's mansion. He was used to getting things done; and there were a number of areas—most notably, civil rights, malapportionment, fairness in criminal justice—where by widespread agreement much remained to be done. Under Warren's leadership, the Court moved from telling the states and the Congress what they could not do to telling them what they must do.

Now we come upon a permanent systemic problem. A court (even a Supreme Court) is not a military junta that governs by fiat. It cannot in fact force many positive actions on many people: it is, Henry Hart wrote, "a tribunal which, after all, does not in the end have the power either in theory or in practice to ram its own personal preferences down other people's throats." Without the collaboration of the other agencies of government, which its decisions may or may not command, the Court cannot make anything happen. (This is why the drives for constitutional amendments fail: there are easier ways to nullify a decision.) An interesting politically neutral example of this problem will arise within the decade in connection with the Penn Central bankruptcy. The Court has permitted the federal government to expropriate the assets that secured loans to the railroad, on the grounds that the creditors can later sue in the Court of Claims. But if the Congress refuses to vote the $10 billion or so that the Court of Claims will award, the Supreme Court will be powerless to get the creditors their money.

A court can identify wrongs, but unless a prohibition will do the trick it must in the end accept whatever remedies are offered by the other governmental organs of a democratic society. Trying to create remedies—an object all sublime for judges as for Gilbert's Mikado—the courts only dig themselves deeper and deeper into the hole. Having determined that a unified nation demanded, though it did not have, a unified commercial code (in *Swift* v. *Tyson* in 1842), the Court wound up insisting that the same set of facts might be covered by two different laws, one for litigants who both lived in the same state and the other for litigants living in different states. Having declared abortion a constitutional right, the courts ultimately find themselves demanding that Catholic doctors and nurses who believe abortions to be murder must perform them anyway or lose federal assistance to their hospitals. (The cases urging this remedy, incidentally, were brought by an organization that calls itself a civil liberties union.) Having determined that the state could not force parents to bus their children away from the neighborhood school to maintain segregation (which is what *Brown* said), the Court eventually compels public agencies to force parents to bus their children away from the neighborhood school to achieve desegregation.

Tocqueville thought it was a good idea to have political disputes settled in courtrooms, but he was wrong, as Taney presently demonstrated in *Dred Scott*, when he wrote the southern states' fugitive slave laws into the Constitution. Justice Jackson observed that because a case cannot be expanded to encompass the realities and concerns of a great nation, those realities and concerns must be shrunk to the compass of a case. A law prohibiting child labor comes to be seen not as social policy to promote the general welfare, but as an abrogation of the right of freedom of contract enjoyed by both the employer and the parents of the child; the question of whether compulsory busing really makes sense is subsumed beneath the injustice done to individual black children by the failings of the slum school; complicated questions of freedom of speech with relation to pornography reduce to opinions that Barney Rosset should not and Ralph Ginsburg should go to jail. The distortions are often extreme, and too many people, nonlawyers as well as lawyers, begin to think that the game played with pieces of paper and words is more important than the activities, customs, hopes, and fears of the humanity that must be excluded.

And speaking as they do ex cathedra—supposedly enforcing great principles rather than making practical adjustments—

appellate courts that have made a mistake have absolutely no dignified way to retreat. It is pretty generally agreed by now that the courts were wrong in the line of school busing decisions that began with the *Charlotte* case and culminated in Judge Garrity's Boston Massacre—but how the courts are to turn around on this issue is by no means clear. The problems are especially difficult when the courts attempt the feat Justice Holmes once derided as "creating fictitious equality when there are real differences." For here we enter the thicket where people who talk equality really mean compensation for natural inequalities, and people who talk justice (as Cardozo noted) really mean charity.

In this focus, the Equal Rights Amendment appears particularly mischievous, because it invites courts to do what in fact they cannot do. Codes to define what constitutes "equality" cannot be drawn up by courts, and case-by-case examination is neither an efficient nor—in truth—a feasible way to answer Freud's question about what these women want. Like the Congress, the women's movement is ducking the hard work of deciding what laws ought to accomplish, assuming that the courts can make not just sense but public policy out of vague statutory language. The courts have real functions to perform in resolving disputes between litigants whose real interests are in conflict; it is improper and ultimately fruitless in a democracy to bring lawsuits "to change the law"—but precisely such lawsuits are invited by the Equal Rights Amendment.

Because the court system's capacity to create useful remedies is so limited, even the activist bench turns out to be really good only at saying NO. In politicized matters then the product of enlarged access to the courts becomes more endless, futile, suffocating delay. The road or shopping center or power plant or factory cannot be built, the license cannot be issued, the housing or sewage project cannot be placed here, the prices cannot be raised (or, in ICC and CAB matters, lowered), the unused trackage cannot be abandoned, the psychopath cannot be kept under lock and key—because the environmental im-

pact statement is inadequate, or there are insufficient assur-
ances that blacks are going to get enough jobs, or the neighborhood has not been adequately consulted about site selection, or
somebody was not given sufficient time to appeal the decision
not to require the hearing examiner to reopen the hearings for
evidence previously excluded, or the judge let the jury see a
picture that police who failed to knock before they entered the
room had taken of the "suspect" bending over the warm corpse
with a dripping knife in his hand. When in the aftermath of the
Arab boycott Congress overruled Judge Skelly Wright's frivolous insistence on blocking construction of the Alaska pipeline
(because the right of way to be granted the builders was a little
larger than that contemplated in a provision of a separate, forgotten law he had discovered), the Sierra Club grudgingly announced that it would not challenge the congressional determination in court, though its attorneys were convinced they could
at least delay the construction of the pipeline another five years
if they chose to bring suit.

In the American system of government, the legislature and
the executive, each in its own way, are to express the popular
will; the courts and the Constitution they enforce are to protect
minority interests from abuse. That is for real; the Common
Cause–Ralph Nader type of lawsuit, which pretends to vindi-
cate the rights of majorities against the governments elected by
those majorities, is not real but symbolic. Judges complain that
these cases are incompetently prepared, but the problem more
often is that they are incompetently conceived: the plaintiffs
have chosen the wrong forum.

Worse, by their reliance on advocacy models and two-party
conflict, such cases poison the wells of government. "This much
I think I know," Learned Hand once wrote, "that a society so
riven that the spirit of moderation is gone, no court *can* save;
that a society where that spirit flourishes, no court *need* save;
that in a society which evades its responsibility by thrusting
upon courts the nurture of that spirit, that spirit in the end will
perish." Yielding to the insistence of the abstraction-oriented

interest groups thrown up as a social byproduct of affluence and education, our courts have allowed themselves to place the perfection of the union and the establishment of justice above the needs of domestic tranquillity, the common defense, the general welfare, and the blessings of liberty. Our history knows no occasion when courts have had the last word in a dispute with the public about the ranking of fundamental goals. Given the need for increasing but subtle government intervention in people's lives in the years ahead (whether that intervention is called "planning" or something else), the courts must become reluctant to take actions that damage the legitimacy of more democratic decision-making procedures. Especially if we can begin jiggering those procedures to make them produce decisions.

3

Daniel Boorstin once suggested that a salient difference between the householder of two generations ago and the householder of today was that early Americanus would come home from church of a Sunday, pick up the paper and browse it, and then hand it over to his wife with the comment that nothing much had happened yesterday. The modern householder will come back from church, pick up the paper, and presently fling it into a corner complaining that this is a lousy newspaper. For the great majority of newspaper readers and television viewers, the drive to catch the news is a subset of the general drive toward boredom reduction that Kierkegaard feared as the basic instinct of civilized man. Robert Burns watching the spider on the prison wall was, Kierkegaard thought, more fortunate than modern (i.e., nineteenth-century) man seeking endless sensation. Affluence has led us to believe that we have a right to a world more *interesting* than the real world.

News is first of all entertainment, but lacking mnemonics or music it tends to be rather unmemorable entertainment. Researchers from the University of Washington report that less than a quarter of the viewers of Seattle's six o'clock news show could remember the lead story of an evening when called back three or four hours later. Still, the fact that people do not remember the news does not keep them from having opinions on any identified question. Market researcher James Vicary while trying out his tools as a young man used to ask respondents their views of the Trade Metallics Act, and in an actual majority of cases would get expressions for or against a mythical law. The real "Don't Know" section is much understated in every public opinion poll.

The background for nearly all political decision in a democracy is formed by this miasma of half-remembered selectively recalled news—which is often enough built on the titillation of catastrophe. There really is no limit to the professional credulity of the press. Early in 1975, there appeared on the front pages of newspapers all over the western world a warning that some motivelessly malignant group might raise the necessary tens of millions of dollars, equip a ship for Antarctic research, spend some months (presumably invisible to patrolling aircraft) drilling through miles of ice to plant nuclear explosives at the bottom of the ice cap and slide it into the ocean for the purpose of raising the sea level and drowning most of the world's population. I waited more or less breathlessly for the movie this fantasy must be announcing—but, no, all the science editors were taking it *seriously;* it had to be an important story, because it got them the front-page space, the sixty-second time slot, which they need to assure their own position in the political struggles of their shop.

" 'It looks to me,' said Mr. Hennessy [at the turn of the century], 'as though this counthry was goin' to the divvle.' 'Put down that magazine,' said Mr. Dooley. 'Now d'ye feel betther? I thought so . . .' " Walter Lippmann in his more sober way, in 1924, expressed the same concern: "If the newspapers, then, are to be charged with the duty of translating the whole public life of mankind, so that every adult can arrive at an opinion on every moot topic, they fail, they are bound to fail, in any future one can conceive they will continue to fail. . . . The press . . . is like the beam of a searchlight that moves restlessly about, bringing one episode and then another out of darkness into vision. Men cannot do the work of the world by this light alone."

It is a peculiarly governmental problem. Businesses have their own sources of information in their markets, and though consumers are all supposed to be patsies for advertising, the fact is that if the product is unsatisfactory they don't buy it again. But the consumer as voter and citizen, and the politician as legislator and officeholder may be highly dependent on news for input to the decision-making processes that increasingly influence all our lives. In another culture, Stanley Morison wrote of *The Times* of London that it "exists to instruct and inform Members of Parliament." News, as Lippmann insisted, simply isn't good enough for that. Justice Jackson's problem recurs in a different context: because the story cannot be expanded to include the great causes and consequences of an event, the causes and consequences must be shrunk to the dimensions of the story. Inaccuracy understates the difficulty (though anyone who has been personally involved in a reported event knows how poor the odds are that he will recognize what he reads about it); the correct word is "inadequacy."

Let us take once again some examples that do not raise high emotional voltages: two economic issues that have been so distorted by conventional reporting that the chances of dealing intelligently with important problems are greatly diminished.

Among the monthly figures that come through the newspapers into books by sociologists and political commentators is the average "net real disposable income" of American workers. This is the paycheck, after all deductions for taxes, adjusted to reflect changes in the cost of living. But there are economic goods purchased collectively by the society through government (via taxes) or through private association (via collective bargaining). Since the 1950s, the more strongly organized American unions have noted that wage increases are effectively diminished by their members' rising income taxes, and have sought to increase the proportion of the total contract package that comes in untaxed "fringe benefits"—medical care, pension plans, life insurance, days off, etc.

These demands are enthusiastically welcomed by members of the management negotiating team, because such benefits won for unionized workers will also be given to executives. (A vice-president with a $60,000 salary, paying taxes on the marginal dollar at 50 percent and stuck with $1,500 worth of medical bills a year, will gain $3,000 worth of benefits from a plan by which the company picks up all medical expenses.) As inflation and increased productivity push American workers into higher tax brackets, their unions arrange for higher proportions of the wages fund to be paid in untaxed fringes. The "tax loophole" of fringe benefits costs the government at least five times as much as the oil depletion allowance ever did.

Meanwhile, due in part to Baumol-Bowen, in part to actual improvements in some services, and in part to greater appropriations for government charity to the poor, the proportion of the GNP taken in taxes has continued to rise. In the early 1960s, about 24 percent of the nation's product went to pay for government; by the early 1970s, that total had passed 31 percent —and in 1975, with production down and public budgets still rising, it unquestionably went over a third. The same commentators who decry the loss of "net real disposable income" demand that high proportions of such increases in government expenditure be paid for through income taxes. But the higher the taxes deducted from the paycheck, obviously, the lower the "net real disposable income." All collective purchasing, through fringe benefits or government, must tend to reduce net real disposable income, which is a measure of individual receipts alone. We cannot conduct public business or construct intelligible tax systems if people insist on using statistics as misleading as "net real disposable income"—but that's what's in the papers.

(Incidentally, in passing, the statistics seem to be misleading even on their own terms: fully employed American workers continued to increase their net real disposable income until 1974. Geoffrey H. Moore of the National Bureau of Economic Research has broken the "average earnings" reported by the Bureau of Labor Statistics into categories for heads of households and others. While the average net earnings for the work force as a whole rose only about a third from 1969 to 1974, no more than matching the increase in the cost of living, the average for "heads of households with full-time jobs" rose about 46 percent, yielding a better than 10 percent rise in purchasing power—despite the simultaneous increase in collective purchasing of fringe benefits and government services.)

On the other side of the economic debate, the *Wall Street Journal* and others have lamented the decrease in profits as a proportion of the GNP—down below 10 percent in 1974, which was a good year for reported profits, from an average range of 12–14 percent in the 1950s. Capital investment, necessary to increase productivity, can derive, the *Journal* argues, only from profits; thus the failure of the system to generate sufficient profits imperils our economic future. This argument is faulty from the beginning, because there is no inherent reason why capital investment cannot be financed from household savings, via the intermediation of the stock market and the underwriters (or even by the government, out of tax revenues, like the great dams and the highway systems and the rivers-and-harbors projects); but the argument fails even on its own terms, because "profits" are calculated only after interest payments on debt. From the 1950s to the present, the ratio of debt to equity in the financing of American business has roughly reversed: one-third used to be debt and two-thirds stock, but now two-thirds is debt. In the early 1960s, the proportion of gross corporate earnings required to pay interest was only about 15 percent; by 1974, it was about 40 percent. If profits were 12 percent of the GNP in 1960, in other words, the total return to capital through profits and interest together ran a little over 14 percent; if profits were 9 percent of GNP in 1974, the total return through profits and interest together approached 15 percent. The worry about the growth of debt in the society is very real; the worry about the apparent decline in "profits," which is merely a subworry of growing debt, should not be placed front and center.

I have used these examples because the demonstration of the difficulty is value-free. The sort of categorical distortions that arise in the presentation of busing, pornography, abortion, crime, pollution, and the like are equally extreme—as is the selective amnesia that, for example, presents the Arab-Israeli conflict in terms of 1947, 1967, and 1973, when the Arabs were the aggressors (the 1967 Israeli strike was clearly defensive in context), and ignores 1956, when the Israelis joined with the British and French in the last hurrah of gunboat imperialism. One likes to assume that legislators, who are paid to pay attention to public matters and have the resources of committee staffs and expert counsel, will know more about any "issue" than appears in the press, but often they do not. And they are subject to pressure from home from people whose acquaintance with what is at stake derives entirely from the news media: viz., Biafra.

Again, the problem is systemic. What's Hecuba to him? asked Hamlet, marveling at the passion of the players; and to this question, rhetorical in Shakespeare, newsmen must find real answers, every day. To the extent that the story deals with a dispute between individuals or organizations, news posits an outside party concerned with how the dispute is resolved: the reader or viewer with his chosen surrogate, the newsman. But it is often true that the only interests significantly involved are those of the disputants (for example, in the annually publicized war between professional athletes and owners over the "reserve clause"), and that the situation can in fact be understood only if it is presented as they see it. In the translation to a "public perspective" required by the obligation of the press to its consumers, the truth of the matter may be discarded.

Where one of the parties to a reported dispute is the government, which is increasingly common (not least because many of the activities of government must be publicized to be effective), the press must assume a stance that treats the "public interest" of the reader or viewer as something different from the public interest expressed by government. This often fictitious third party ("you") is among the major sources of distrust of government, and its presence in the news reports ultimately gives birth to real organizations (Nader's, Common Cause, and the like) that claim to embody it. Foundations, which will assume this mantle themselves whenever they can, are delighted to pay the bills. I am not (God forbid) arguing that government is always deserving of public trust; only that the presumption that it is never deserving imposes losses as well as gains.

My hunch is that the increasing seriousness of approach in the news media has made these problems worse. A. J. Liebling recalled that a boss in the Hearst organization once told him, "The public is interested in just three things: Blood, money, and the female organ of sexual intercourse." When the newspapers were devoted mostly to inconsequent sensationalism, those people who were interested in more important matters would choose for themselves what seemed significant in the much less salient presentation of unsensational events. Now the newspaper and television editors presume to decide what is important to the public out of the welter of nonboring "news." We have not necessarily gained by the change.

We stand at one of the intersection points of affluence (with its accompanying education) and technology. People want their newspapers and broadcasters to keep them informed of what is important in the world, and both the geographical and incidental range of what seems important to newspaper readers has been immensely expanded. But a newspaper is inescapably about what happened *yesterday*. E. M. Forster in his lectures on the novel sighs that yes, alas!, the novel tells a story; and the newspaper and the news show, alas!, tell you what's new. And what's new is by no means necessarily what's important.

The great loss is the sense of history, and it has been creeping up on us for a very long time. Since Brunelleschi learned how "they" had built the Pantheon and bettered the accomplishment of the ancients with his Duomo in Florence, European man has felt less and less awe of his ancestors. The American from the start (like the Cuban or the Chinese today) considered himself a "new man." But there is no new man—just the same old sack of ordure, en route to becoming ashes and dust.

Our time horizons are always much higher looking backward than they can ever be looking ahead. When we lose the habit of looking backward, we lose the sense of what it really means to create a future. "To know what is permanent in our own ideals and desires," Harold Laski said in his inaugural lecture as the first professor of political science at the London School of Economics, "we must know what they have meant in the experience of men. Man, if I may invert the famous aphorism of Rousseau, is born everywhere in chains, and he becomes free only upon the grim condition of self-knowledge. A true politics . . . is above all a philosophy of history."

Because the news has no historical memory, the newspaper has no predictive capability—even in the short run. As these pages are written, the *New York Times* seems to have put a stop to its prize-winning year-long chain of fright stories about how population has already outrun grain production; and one of these days, sooner or later, the *Times* will be carrying stories about the greatest wheat glut in history, no place to put the stuff (though in India and elsewhere people will still be starving). One can be certain that the stories about the glut will make little reference to the many stories about the dearth. Nothing was more fundamental to human knowledge of the world than the idea that there were fat years and lean years (remember Joseph and the Pharaoh); but even that understanding can be lost through the combination of affluence, technology, and newspapers.

There is thus a conflict between the newspapers' and broadcasters' roles in the legitimation of leadership (which can and should be judged by recent performance) and in the legitimation of the questions to be answered by a society (which must be judged by their future significance). The unfortunate compromise sends the papers (and the television news shows) in search of new faces who can be presented as emerging leaders, embodying forthcoming debates. One cannot entirely deny Spiro Agnew's well-publicized objection to the extensive coverage given meaningless figures like George Lincoln Rockwell and Huey P. Newton, but the news editors have a problem: given the entertainment expectations of their readers and viewers, they can deal with the future they wish to include in their bailiwick only by personalizing it.

The worry usually expressed is that media packagers will take a pretty face, set it properly in the studio, and peddle the fake product on television to bemused voters. I do not think people can be deceived that way. The more serious worry, for me, is the incessant partially subconscious judging of potential public figures by the degree to which they are or are not "interesting," the constant choice by public figures of issues on which to speak according to their judgment of what is or is not "newsworthy." The worst government of all would be government by celebrity, the worst waste of limited decision-making resources would be primacy for those questions that are most salient in the press. But a democratic society in our state of technology is forever being irritated by messages from the machinery of mass communications, and to soothe the body politic it becomes increasingly necessary to apply the remedies where the irritations itch.

A few years ago, a member of the science and technology section of the Congressional Reference Service noted in passing that the great task before American government in the last quarter of this century would be "the development of suitable disincentives to live in the urban corridors." This is, at a minimum, *one* of the great tasks; but a government officer who decides what he should be working on by reference to the stories in today's paper or on tonight's news show could never get started on it. News impinges on the allocation of time; when political leadership allots time to one "issue" rather than another, the opportunity costs can be high.

It was profoundly discouraging to see the presidential campaign of 1976 begin in the press in January 1975—almost a year earlier than any previous campaign had been acknowledged by an important candidate. The premature vote gathering was in part an artifact of the ill-thought law that "reformed" presidential campaign financing by making public funds available to those who could show at least a certain minimal level of prior public support; but it also derived from the instinctual behavior of both newspaper editors and broadcasters, to seek the biggest hook on which to hang any given story. The influence of this incessant campaigning on the work of the Senate was so disruptive that Senator Thomas McIntyre of New Hampshire proposed half-seriously a new rule that would prohibit any candidate for president from introducing a bill; the influence on the interrelations of news and politics may be even more damaging.

No nation can afford to choose its leaders by their quality as campaigners. The old system of huge campaign contributions had grown too corrupt to be tolerated, but at least it tapped into the network of trust and judgment in widening circles of people who knew the candidates. To the extent that future leadership will rise to the top through its capacity to make news, we had better look all the more carefully to the construction of quasi-automatic devices—political mechanisms designed to work as much as possible like market mechanisms—that diminish the significance of deliberate decision-making.

Government in secret is terribly dangerous; government in public is impossible. Our time has not found its middle way. The answer when discovered, I suspect, will be greater emphasis on plan and performance—and Lord knows this leaves a central function for an independent and aggressive press, a careful and able (but, please, not brilliant) judiciary. The old-fashioned journalistic and legal training was more useful than today's sophistication, for if you don't get the details right you can't get anything right. It is when the government is doing something but does not understand the significance of what it is doing that the press and the courts have their most important role to play. Vietnam and Watergate will do as illustrations. In our time, in public and private organizations both, it is not power but incompetence that tends to corrupt; and absolute incompetence corrupts absolutely.

9

And Where Do We Go from Here?

Health is not conscious of itself, but frees the mind for the perception of other things; and even the joy of health, when it comes to the surface, comes rather in the form of some generous enthusiasm for nature, for sport, or for loveable people. So the health of society does not express itself in public opinion but in public affections, in a general enhanced vitality in all the arts, without controversial theories about them. But when society is deeply troubled, when men do not know what to do, what to think, what to enjoy, or how to avoid hateful compulsions, then every complaint and every panacea gathers adherents, parties arise, and ideologies fill the atmosphere with their quarrels. . . . All these ideologies are too superficial and these men too commonplace to make much difference in the natural course of events, upward or downward, as the circumstances of the age may determine. For there are real revolutions in things, migrations, and confusion of peoples, decay and invention in the arts, intensification or disappearance of commerce: and on such real mutations the ideas and the shouts of the public play a thin and inconstant treble.

—*George Santayana*

1

One of the best teachers I visited during my years in the galleys of elementary and secondary education was a junior high school science specialist who had adorned the front of his room with a wall-to-wall banner that hung just over the blackboard. Neatly painted on the cloth, in an enlarged italic hand, was a statement of the one certain and demonstrable truth we have: "THIS TOO," the banner read, "SHALL PASS." Dr. Lewis Thomas has suggested that doctors' children take fewer prescription medicines than laymen's children, because when they get sick their fathers give them a hot drink and an aspirin and tell them to go to bed. "The great secret, known to internists and learned early in marriage by internists' wives . . . is that most things get better by themselves. Most things, in fact, are better by morning." It is not true that there is a remedy for every evil under the sun; and for a good proportion of the evils we would like to remedy, the best cure—the only known cure—is time.

Even if there were a remedy for every evil, I would not be the man who knew it. I wholeheartedly affirm that decisions about what to do next should be made only in consultation with groups, not by individuals. Reality excludes options, because what has happened can no longer be otherwise (and reality of course implies the past made present). Thus an individual can by working at it gather information, analyze, and even explain, all by himself. But the range of consequences of an action undertaken now—and out in the schematic but inescapable world of the second derivative, the later consequences of these consequences—simply cannot be seen in a wide enough focus from a single point of view.

For some of the specific proposals in the pages that follow, then, I have used the formulation "I want," because I learned long ago that I don't always get what I want, that other people want things other than those I want, that I may be wrong, they may be wrong, we may all be wrong. I could not skin a cat if my life depended on it, and the idea of doing so I find more than a little sickening—but I am willing to accept the folk wisdom that there are lots of ways to do it. Not an infinite number of ways, though: there are always principles and procedures worth learning.

The informing principle in all that follows is that the role of government is to tilt the landscape, to help the water run downhill, not to reverse the waterfall. Government probably can't make water run uphill—not every day, anyway—and if it could, the waste of energy and human resources in the process would be devastating to society. For all the violence of its police forces and taxing powers, the pervasiveness of the communications network it dominates, the capabilities of its monitoring technology, modern government is not in fact all that effective.

A very popular story tells of Harry Truman's sympathy for the plight of his incoming successor—poor Ike, he was used to giving orders and having them carried out; now he was going to be president and he'd find that he'd give an order and nothing, absolutely nothing, would happen. People protect themselves. Bureaucracies protect themselves. Over a period of time, what happens results not from great decisions taken with solemn ceremony at the center of power (each letter of the president's name signed with a separate pen, to multiply the souvenirs) but from the multitude of small decisions taken with greater or lesser care by individuals and small organizations scattered all over the landscape. A "tyranny of small decisions," the physicist Alvin Weinberg once called it. And these small decisions are almost always guided, consciously or otherwise, by people's perceptions of their individual or group self-interest.

No doubt there are periods on the S-curve of a revolution when the exhortations of the leader produce enthusiastic cooperation with even the most insane demands from on high (the Cuban intellectuals marching out to chop sugar cane could be the stereotype). But eventually a successful policy must command not obedience nor even cooperation but self-impelled supportive action (if you are serious about getting all that cane cut you had better find material rewards to supplement the psychic satisfactions).

Law enforces habit: people obey laws mostly because on balance it's less trouble to do so. When it becomes more trouble, they stop obeying. As the Russians have been learning (and as Mao feared), affluence increases people's ability to ignore the law much faster than technology improves the state's capacity to enforce it. The more productive the individual, the greater the assumption of his "worth," independent, somehow, of his society. In America, left and right vie to see which can make greater claims for the individual as against the collectivity. Except in our rhetoric, we concede that men are controlled not by law, nor by faith nor hope nor charity, but by greed. So be it: I agree, because I do not think it can be any other if men are to be free.

How tightly greed controls behavior in any society is likely to be a function of technology. The military-agricultural complex of the late Middle Ages, as Karl Marx and Richard Wagner realized, interposed established restraints between greed and its objects: "The vassal class created by the military mutation of the eighth century," to take Lynn White's formulation, "never lost completely its sense of noblesse oblige." Then the modern world—our world—came to pass: "a new and rival class of burghers revived the Roman notion of the unconditional and socially irresponsible possession of property." It remains true that the sharing activities (from chamber music to football) are among the great pleasures of human society, but they are not central to it. Even among Wagner's grail seekers and Marx's communists, individual greed is always one of the prime movers; at best, it is mediated through less distasteful disguises. The taproot of modernity (from survival of the fittest to Better Red Than Dead) is the belief that self-sacrifice must be neurotic. The virtue of it is that greeds are fundamentally commensurate: one individual's can check another's without shattering the loser. Thus, greed itself is best controlled by countervailing greed.

The principle works very effectively if you can structure the situation to apply it. In the early years of this century, much American manufacturing was carried on in dangerous loft buildings with minimal protection against fire. The horror story of the Triangle Fire produced legislation, but the legislation was not in fact very effective: nothing that depends upon government inspection and policing for its enforcement is likely to be effective. (Even today, a New York City code for alterations in duct work on skyscrapers, hastily written in response to the reality of several near disasters and the fashionable interest in catastrophe per se, has simply been ignored as impractical by most owners of buildings.) What made the difference between the fire-prone factory of the turn of the century and the fire-proof factory of today was the development of fire insurance, and the insistence of the banks that business places be adequately insured before the banks would risk their money in loans. The factory owner could no longer save money by cutting corners on safety, because his insurance premium would go up drastically (if he could get insurance at all); the insurance company was stimulated to inspect effectively because its profits depended on minimizing losses.

The fire insurance example is particularly nice because everything locks together so neatly: the profit-seeking discretion of the manufacturers is policed by the greed of the casualty insurance company, which is in turn policed by the prudence of the bank. No doubt, insurance models are limited in their applicability and work best when the person buying the insurance has other reasons to take whatever steps may be necessary to reduce the chance of the accident against which the insurance has been purchased. Moreover, government subsidy that removes the incentive to minimize outlays may frustrate the police functions of insurance schemes—viz., the relationship of Medicare and Blue Cross. Nevertheless, the insurance device is capable of extension much beyond its current uses.

Home-mortgage insurance (government-invented but now mostly private) makes it possible for ordinary people to buy houses at interest rates comparable to or better than those paid by large industrial companies. Title insurance has healed what was once a running sore in American real property law and custom. The new pension reform law backs up the employee's vested right to a pension through a governmental insurance system which ultimately will vary its rates according to the adequacy of the individual pension plan; and meanwhile private insurers have begun to police the behavior of the pension trustees. The muncipal bond insurers, springing up in the after-math of the New York City disaster, have already had a whole-some influence on municipal finances.

Left alone by the state insurance departments, the insurance companies through rate setting might considerably diminish the incidence of automobile accidents and of medical malprac-tice (though it would mean a number of drivers and doctors would be unable to afford their licenses). A really major differ-ence in life insurance rates between smokers and nonsmokers (policed by the right of the company to reduce benefits if the insured can be shown to have cheated on his nonsmoking decla-ration) would probably slow the rise of cigarette consumption that has made the anti-tobacco legislation of the 1960s look so futile. Occupational safety factors other than fire should also be controllable by insurance companies, and I suspect that consid-erable value can be got from insurance structures in the pollu-tion area, too. Recent years have seen a growth of interest in publicly financed insurance for the victims of crime. If the premiums for such insurance were assessed by experience against the real estate ratables of the areas where the crime occurs, the cities would light the streets better and take their policing obligations more seriously.

2

Ideally, a highly developed capitalist society should generate structures of incentives that make price/cost signals responsive to needs that are determined politically as well as to needs that are determined by individual immediate choice. Where such incentives (and penalties) do not arise spontaneously through enterprise, the highest function of government is to create them, to rest an official, ponderable, but not too heavy hand on the scales as a replacement for Adam Smith's invisible hand, which in modern societies has lost some of its skill.

Among the most obvious ways to harness greed is to vary the

"tax consequences" of private action. Much of what American government does already falls under this rubric, some of it consciously, some of it by inadvertence. Capital investment is directly stimulated by tax credits. Home ownership as opposed to renting is furthered by the homeowner's right to deduct from taxable income the interest on his mortgage and his real estate tax payments. The oil companies (and some others) are encouraged to explore for new sources of supply by tax laws which permit the writing off of search and development costs as they are incurred (though manufacturers can write off the costs of their factories only through gradual depreciation; developers of geothermal energy sources complain bitterly that the tax law treats them as it treats manufacturers rather than as it treats oil companies, and thus impedes the exploitation of new sources of power). Contributions to educational and medical and artistic causes are boosted by the charitable deduction, which in effect makes the government a partner in the generosity of the rich. Long before there was revenue sharing, the federal government contributed several billion dollars a year in tax exemptions for state and municipal bond interest, to encourage individuals to invest in the extension of public services in their own localities. Without the cost-free risk premiums of the exemption, New York City could never have borrowed more money than it can hope to repay; and without the deduction of interest payments from profits subject to taxation, American industry would never have developed the top-heavy debt structure that threatens our future prosperity.

Tax consequences may have other unintended results. The progressive income tax system promotes cohabitation as against marriage when the two partners are both employed at relatively similar salaries: by filing separate returns, they incur lesser total tax liabilities than they would suffer if they had to pool their income for tax purposes through holy matrimony. (And social security procedures promote cohabitation rather than marriage by retired widows and widowers.) Tax arithmetic in an age of increasing female employment has been more persuasive than some more advertised psychosocial factors, I think, in producing the rising number of young couples who live together without getting married. If only one has an income, marriage yields the better tax return, and in fact the unsanctioned "marriage" is much less common among one-income couples.

Because people are more likely to fight against their own punishment than against their neighbor's rewards, tax penalties are more difficult to organize than tax breaks. To this writing, no congressional committee has been willing even to schedule hearings on something so obviously necessary as excise taxes on automobiles geared to their size and energy efficiency. (Instead, we hope to impose efficiency as we imposed clean emissions, through legislated arbitrary "standards"; some people never learn.) A degree of moral disapproval is usually required to impose tax penalties in the face of the normal presumption for equality of treatment: cigarettes and alcohol can be taxed heavily because they're bad for you (even though such taxes are perhaps the most regressive on the books: cost per dose will not keep most poor people from consuming tobacco or booze). But taxes designed to discourage certain activities are certainly necessary weapons in our future. Effluent taxes are far and away the best device for reducing pollutants, and high taxes on profits from the sale of land will be necessary if we are to have the ghost of a chance of saving our cities or the farmland near them.

Tax benefits are a honey pot that draws too many undesirable animals; tax penalties produce swarms of lawyers, accountants, and bribe givers, redefining terms, recalculating the books, corrupting the tax collectors. Moreover, because both benefits and penalties seek to influence behavior rather indirectly, they often yield unexpected consequences that drastically distort the original intent of the preference or punishment. Tax breaks for home builders led not to the rehousing of the poor but to the spread of second homes and vacation condominiums in the sunshine states. Tax assessments on railroad rights of way (more than reasonable, considering the noise, pollution, blight, and danger caused by railroads running through the heart of town) turned out to give the trucking industry an insuperable advantage over the railroads. You can never do just one thing . . .

Direct payment by the government for what the government wants will often be better procedure than any tax scheme, however imaginative. By influencing the price/cost signals everyone receives, the government communicates its intentions more efficiently than it can if lawyers are needed to explain to their clients what the tax law means. Even during wartime, price signals may be the most effective way for a government to communicate. Political scientist Norton Long—whose instincts were all for government by rule or regulation—once told the story of how the armed services in World War II got the great quantity of fractional horsepower motors they needed to turn gun turrets and the like. First manufacturers were ordered to increase their output. They complained they didn't have enough skilled workers to do so, and their work force was thereupon exempted from the draft. They insisted that they didn't have the steel and other raw materials required by the production process, and they were awarded special allocations of scarce commodities. Still not enough motors. "Finally," Long recalled, "somebody said, 'Let's double the price,' and within months we had more fractional horsepower motors than we could use." And excess profits taxes got most of the money back to the government.

The great advantage of direct payment procedures is that they accomplish the mission. Housing and hospitals and roads actually get built, satellites fly, businesses directly subsidized to do so will hire and train previously unemployable youngsters, the state university medical school does turn out doctors to work in the home state, the wires criss-cross the countryside to bring electricity to the farmhouses. Direct purchasing by the government, however, raises the specter of opportunity costs in ways that tax decisions do not—the budget must allocate to one purpose rather than another—and advertising becomes necessary to sell the program. The immediate result is what Aaron

Wildavsky, dean of the school of government at the University of California, bitterly describes as "the 'great-leap-forward psychology,' combining undue pessimism about the past with wild optimism about the future." In this atmosphere, crookedness and cost overruns become the norm, as we have repeatedly seen in the Defense Department as well as in the poverty program and the housing programs.

3

All political philosophies are more or less a cargo cult, an assertion of faith that somehow government can see to it that we will all get something for nothing. It never works out right, because there really is no free lunch. One way or another, the members of a society pay for everything their society gets, even those goods on which "you can't put a dollars-and-cents price." Thus the central question to be asked about any proposal for government intervention in private activity is not whether it is "fair" but whether it promotes or retards the general interest.

In this context, the great reform needed in American government is the substitution of a value added tax (VAT), improved from the European model, for perhaps half of the present corporate income tax. Few taxes are so thoroughly counterproductive as a 48 percent corporate income tax. It encourages waste, because the government picks up half the cost of company planes and limousines, fancy entertainment, executive bonuses, lobbying, institutional advertising, and the like. Because interest payments on debt are deductible from taxable corporate income but dividend payments on stock are not, the tax encourages corporations to finance expansion or modernization from the sale of bonds rather than the sale of stock, making the economy at once less adaptable, less liquid, and less venturesome. Because stock prices are a function of reported post-tax income, accountants and lawyers are stimulated to invent all sorts of ways to rig corporate books to make income look lower or higher, depending on need in this quarter, and several professions are corrupted simultaneously. Because corporations have such good reason to lie, government planners can never really find out what is going on (the inventory figures solemnly presented and analyzed in the papers, for example, are in large part lies corrected by guesswork). And it is simply silly to say that the public does not pay corporate income tax: like other costs, it shows up in prices. The only thing to be said for a corporate income tax—and the reason for retaining it at a reduced level—is that this tax is one of the most effective of the automatic stabilizers: the fact that today's losses can be deducted from subsequent profits for tax purposes encourages a man to continue through hard times.

The value added tax, a central part of the economic organization of the European Common Market, is a tax on production processes. The difference between the cost of materials purchased and the finished sale price is the added value, and a tax is assessed on that benefit from production at every stage: the steel mill pays on the difference between the iron and coal cost and the price of the ingot; the steel fabricator pays on the difference between the cost of the ingot and the price of the finished beam; the road builder pays on the difference between the price of the beam and the concrete and the price of the bridge. From the consumer's point of view, of course, VAT is a sales tax like any other; but it is a lot more manipulable than a sales tax.

Through VAT, the Baumol-Bowen dilemma can be resolved. To pay for increasingly expensive medical services, education, and the arts through taxes assessed on the entire income of the society is over the long term a hopeless effort, because people will not pay income taxes of such dimensions. But if service production is exempted from VAT (as it is not, incidentally, in Europe), then the net effect is to keep the prices of goods and services in more traditional balance despite the greater benefit to goods production from technological advance. Even in Europe, the delivery of services by government is helped by

VAT, because government production, of course, pays no taxes.

Meanwhile, government should greatly increase the proportion of its tax take represented by land taxes. Henry George had his faults, but his insights remain useful. Land in cities and residential suburbs is the deadest form of wealth, and should not be permitted to become a subject of speculation. In principle, the value of land should be assessed for taxes as though it were being used for the purposes that would give it the highest value, encouraging the most efficient employment of the most monopolistic resource. (There is, after all, only one piece of land in one place.) Thus the land below a block of six-story tenements might be assessed for tax purposes as though it held a twenty-story apartment building, to encourage the construction of the apartment building. Poor people living in such tenements could be subsidized directly from the proceeds of the tax, if public policy called for that. Detached suburban houses would pay considerably more tax than they do today, because the lots on which they stand would carry a much heavier tax burden. On the other hand, the land itself would then be cheaper, and other taxes, falling upon human activity in ways less relevant to the promotion of public purpose, would be correspondingly reduced.

The central purpose of a heavy land tax is to capture for public use the profits on increases in the value of land. When this increased value is the result of publicly financed activity (the construction of a road or transit facility or government office complex or arts center), it is nothing less than shocking that the owners of adjacent land should reap windfall profits. By extension, landowners have no celestial right to gain by the actions of private enterprise that owns and improves adjacent property. By depressing property prices, high land taxes encourage building and—as the interestingly eccentric economist Mason Gaffney insists—more rapidly return to the income stream the capital sunk in construction.

What makes land taxes especially attractive in an era of necessary government intervention is the ease with which they can be used to stimulate desirable activity and discourage undesirable activity. Owners would seek instead of shun landmark designation for their property, or down-zoning to prevent unsocial exploitation, because the reduction in the use-value of the land would also reduce taxes. Farms can be preserved as farms even in areas close to cities by removing them entirely from the tax rolls as long as the farmer continues to farm and own them: because taxes would increase so greatly if the land were taken for other uses, developers would be unable to bid enough to make a sale profitable to the farmer. Meanwhile, housing construction could be subsidized by refunding to the builder on completion and sale of an approved project some previously announced fraction of the land taxes paid during the period of planning and construction; and home ownership could be subsidized by giving new housing temporary relief from land taxes.

Over the last quarter of a century, the home buyer could count on an appreciation of his property over the first five years of his ownership; indeed, such profits were so common that Congress extended capital gains taxes to the sale of residences, which had previously been exempt from such taxation. Given the likelihood of continuing inflation and another ten years of a high rate of household formation, this condition is likely to persist. By excusing the underlying land from taxation for, say, five years—probably on a declining scale of exemption from year to year—government can in effect transfer back to the time of construction and first sale the windfall gains that used to accrue to the homeowner as he moved out. As a "shallow" subsidy, temporarily excused land taxes would be inexpensive to government. And if the taxes were high enough, the two-part stimulus to building would be very effective.

Though effluent taxes are clearly the best way to stimulate the creation of pollution-control devices—and to pay for cleaning up the mess of pollution that has not been controlled—a hefty land tax with exemptions for certain uses could be a major stimulus to the capital investment that is required when the pollution results from industrial production. Nor is the device necessarily restricted to such obvious applications. If the decision is made to encourage the practice of medicine through Health Maintenance Organizations, for example, land used as HMO offices or clinics could be exempted from tax while land used for the practice of medicine by other means remained subject to it. In general, we are talking about the use of the tax system to reallocate costs in the marketplace, about a purposive interpenetration of government and private economic decision. No doubt there would be losses both in what economists would regard as productive efficiency and in what political scientists would consider government effectiveness. But it is in the creation of such interpenetrations that the possibility of a free, productive, rational future society resides.

All such schemes face the danger that government bodies will seek to milk the cow beyond its capacity to produce. If land taxes are to be varied for purposes of stimulus and restraint, governments must be forbidden to take the full revenues that could be available from them. Some requirement limiting the maximum assessment of land taxes to some fraction of potential —and of VAT to levels which permit continuing rewards for technological innovation—must be built into such laws before they are thrown in gear. And, as with any government activity, the new taxes will need constant monitoring by legislators and (with luck) by an informed press. There must also be abort mechanisms that put a stop to the system quickly if it turns out to be promoting corruption and misallocation of resources.

I think the job is do-able, which is not the same thing as saying I think it will be done. To go way out and for the first time in these pages write about things that are certainly not going to happen, I want a National Land Tax with proceeds earmarked for revenue sharing. I want Congress to determine how much in total is to be raised by this tax, and to establish national guidelines for the proportionate shares to be borne by industrial, commercial, residential, recreational, agricultural, and resource-producing land. Then I want regional agencies empowered to alter these ratios for their own areas (subject to review), and to determine the allocation of the resulting revenues according to the size of the service package to be funded by each local jurisdiction. Finally, I want more or less local agencies (perhaps two hundred for the country as a whole), controlled by elected officials, required to raise given sums by category to minimize the economic impact of voting blocs, but given considerable flexibility to assure the consonance of the taxing pattern with desirable land-use patterns. Among the required purposes should be the promotion of integrated housing. The decision about the use of the revenues allocated from the regional agency would be made, as now, by elected local officials; presumably, these officials would thus be more intimately involved with spending than with taxing decisions, and would be more popular with their constituents, which would facilitate recruiting a higher level of talent to local government.

Continuing my fantasy, I want a National Value Added Tax Agency, Congress to determine the total to be raised and establish guidelines for assessing relative burdens, the agency to modify these guidelines at the margin and levy taxes with reference to the expected economic health of each main industry group in the year ahead. Before the actual imposition of the taxes, a monitor unit of the agency and a congressional committee charged with its supervision should agree on trigger points in market activity that would force a change in strategy, and I do mean force. And I want the distribution of these revenues allocated by annually adjusted formula—with discretion for the agency inside the formula—to significant service production that cannot pay its own way, especially education, scientific and medical research, health care for the chronically ill, and the arts.

I want a thorough restructuring of taxation on investment, with stockholders to pay personal taxes on the earnings of the corporations in which they hold shares rather than on the dividends alone (this is a Swiftian modest proposal that would have profound systemic impact, shifting ownership of equity to lower-income levels, charitable endowments, pension and insurance funds, etc.); and with capital gains taxes eliminated entirely to facilitate the free flow of capital to emerging industrial activity. Then I want tax credits which would also flow to the individual investor rather than to the corporation—credits that would apply not across the board to all industrial enterprise but only to those chosen by regulatory agencies, subject to the consent of the appropriate congressional committee. These credits would encourage not only the investment of resources in industrial growth by the companies involved, but the movement of funds from the public to these companies rather than to less productive investment: the government's thumb on the scale. Here again, I want trigger points: if a tax subsidy considered sufficient to stimulate investment in housing or solar energy turns out not to be sufficient, I want a presumption that the market (which expresses the views of so many more people) knows something that has escaped the attention of the bureaucracy and the legislature.

How to divide all such functions among the differing levels of government is a difficult but not impossible question, which I gladly leave to those more skilled in intergovernmental analysis than I will ever be. (I suspect there is something to John Fischer's "development districts" in his book *Vital Signs, U.S.A.*) How to force the agencies and legislative bodies to make their decisions rapidly is a question that can probably be answered by statute, giving an appellant the right to go ahead on his own—refusing to pay a tax or billing the government for a credit—if his appeal is not answered within, say, ninety days. If a high degree of legislative oversight is guaranteed—perhaps by provisions that would compel the agencies to submit their annual work programs and policy directives in some detail for legislative review on a date certain, with legislative assent or amendment required within a limited time—the laws can probably be written in ways that would prevent the courts from interfering with the work of the agencies on grounds that they were not carrying out legislative intent (and it is these grounds, not constitutional grounds, that support most of the decisions by which today's courts prevent necessary governmental flexibility).

One element of totalitarian society can, I think, be imported, under constitutional safeguards, to American government: the occasional plebiscite, as a means of overcoming the bias toward negativism built into representative democracy. Acceptance of the disciplines involved in membership in the Common Market was hard for large numbers of Englishmen, but this was a decision that had to be taken, once and for all, and removed from the normal political arena. While the referendum campaign on this issue was no model of anything, the results did lance a sore that otherwise might have festered for years. In the affluent society, pressures against necessary action (for fuel conservation, for example) may make it impossible for representatives in sufficient numbers to take the political risks without the formal support of a voting majority that has been informed by an open national debate. Public opinion polls without the debate to concentrate people's attention are obviously worthless. The Swiss make referenda work pretty well, and perhaps we can, too—so long as everyone understands that the plebiscite is not democracy in action but a device for the occasional necessary suppression of minority power on the relatively few issues where a minority's rights should not exceed its numerical strength.

4

None of this can work without widespread understanding that no complicated society can be run by "the rule of law." All government activity must be discretion-oriented rather than rule-bound; and the word "planning" should rarely be used without the modifying phrase "for contingencies."

More terrifying than the economic downturn of 1974–75 was the revelation of the total lack of preparation for such an event at every level of American government, despite the inevitability that a deep recession would occur someday and the evidence throughout late 1973 and early 1974 that it was coming soon. You didn't have to know much to know there was major trouble ahead, especially but not exclusively in automobiles and construction; but apparently you had to know more than American government (or banking) knew.

In January 1975, with consumer confidence at its ebb and the economy in the steepest part of its decline, about a third of the American work force took a cut in its take-home pay, and employers who had to debate whether their revenues could justify their current employment expenditures saw the costs of their payrolls rise. This horror was perpetrated by the normal working out of the social security tax system, which assessed payroll taxes of 11.7 percent, equally divided between employer and employee, on salaries up to $12,400 a year. Everyone who made more than that in 1974 had seen his salary check rise once he had earned $12,400 for the year to date, only to find it diminished again with the arrival of the new year. And employers whose payroll-related obligations to the government had been reduced toward the end of the year by the elimination of tax on employees earning more than $12,400 a year found their costs boosted by reimposed payroll taxes.

Now, there was no sense to this at all. There is no reason why the social security tax system should not have been designed to spread the taxable year over the real year, rather than starting everybody out afresh on January 1. The work force could easily be divided into ten equal groups according to the last digit in each social security number, and the start of each individual's year would then occur in one of the first ten months. (November and December could be eliminated as start-up months to preserve payrolls for Christmas shopping.) Even in the preposterous system we had, it would have made sense in January 1975 to postpone the reimposition of social security taxes on higher income employees, preserving their take-home pay at the moment of most severe decline in the economy, at the expense of restricting it toward the end of the year, when in everyone's expectations the economy would be in recovery.

Indeed, there would have been little if any loss to the government in a general reduction of withholding taxes in early 1975. The great majority of workers qualify for income tax rebates when they complete their returns. A reduction in withholding rates in the first quarter of 1975 would have put money in people's pockets without necessarily reducing in the slightest the actual government tax collections over the period 1975–76: in most cases, the government could have regained in reduced spring 1976 rebates what it lost in reduced early 1975 collections. Having given an immediate boost to a falling economy, government could then have decided at leisure how much should be tax reduction, and how much should be tax postponement.

These examples of inflexibility touch merely upon the lack of authority in American government to exercise discretion when discretion is needed. Nobody had to do much work to know that demand should be stimulated by tax reduction at the beginning of 1975: all the debate that delayed the actual delivery of the medicine was about details. But in fact tax reductions of the dimensions finally awarded were not wise policy in early 1975. We adopted them—and this is what was finally terrifying—because we had literally no alternatives. All the other interventions that could have been available if somebody had done the basic work of government were not to be found even on the horizons of plausibility.

"Planning," whatever the word means, is inescapable in human society beyond the nomad stage. Every farmer "plans," and so of course does the utility company building a nuclear reactor to come on line in 1983, and the government that establishes a Medicare system. John Kenneth Galbraith, our leading advocate of greater planning, has divided the American economy into two sectors, planned and unplanned, and argued that the planned sector does very well and the unplanned sector rather poorly. The fact that the most highly planned sectors were the worst sufferers in 1973–75—utilities, automobiles, retail chains, airlines—has not for a moment dampened the enthusiasm for this argument.

What is usually meant by people who demand more "planning" in American society is an enforcement machinery that would make all private plans subservient to one big public plan. Exactly how this master plan is to be constructed is not specified; presumably, a lot of economics professors would be recruited to the civil service. Wassily Leontief and Leonard Woodcock, urging Congress to pass a law that would mandate national planning, admit that much better information would have to be gathered before the scheme could become operational. But the only reliable source of economic information is the marketplace, which the planners would distort unpredictably in the act of planning. The French Commissariat du Plan is much admired, and with reason—the satellite cities now springing up around the Ile de France and the modernization of the hinterlands would have been much harder to accomplish without the capital set aside for this purpose through the Plan —but the people who work there are the first to say that when final decisions about what, where, and when are to be made, nobody pays any attention at all to the Plan: the feel of the market sets most of the priorities.

The problem in America is that government expectations are based on business plans, and because business and government agree, nobody develops *contingency* plans. If it turns out that individuals do not behave as predicted, nobody has any ideas about what to do next. But the difficulty of predicting the behavior of human individuals—even in groups—is not resolved by our technology. The most experienced consumer-goods manufacturer with the biggest research department still comes up a loser in the large majority of his new-product introductions. The CANCEL key on the computer terminal is even more important than the eraser on the other end of the pencil.

The point of government planning is to be ready when what you expect does not happen. The man-on-the-moon program worked because there were so many moments in the countdown when corrections could be introduced if errors emerged. Obviously, nobody could, should, or did plan for 9.5 percent unemployment in spring 1975; but government (and to a lesser extent industry) could and should have planned actions to be taken *if* there was 9.5 percent unemployment in spring 1975, despite plans to the contrary. Instead, observers were confronted with a government that could do nothing but cut taxes, stimulating demand in general, when the obvious need was for government purchasing and specific subsidy, creating demand for certain goods and services.

The children of the baby boom are growing up and forming households, yet the construction of new housing in 1974–75 fell below the level required for replacement of deteriorated existing stock. Private and public agencies established to plan our way out of the energy crisis were stressing the urgent need for greater electric power production to relieve dependence on oil in the period around and after 1980, yet utilities all over the country were abandoning or postponing their plans to construct new facilities, because they couldn't raise the money or the environmentalists were blocking the sites. The failure to complete the interstate highway system and the decay of the railroad track beds serving the cities were hastening the process of urban abandonment, yet the environmentalists and communards were preventing the construction of urban highways and the industrial infrastructure needed to repair the tracks was not even on the drawing boards. Unemployment and underutilization of productive facilities in the construction industries was at a rate of at least 25 percent, next to the automobile disaster the worst drag on the economy. Surely there should have been in bureau drawers in government offices fully worked out plans for building or subsidizing (or both) housing projects, power plants, roads, and railroad lines—but the bureau drawers were empty. Even if Congress had been ready to appropriate money for such productive purposes, it could not have been spent, because the "planning" had not been done. And to get started on such projects after the recession was upon us would guarantee that the new government-financed construction got under way in the recovery phase of the cycle, when it would only boost prices and create shortages.

The danger that the altered automobiles required by the Environmental Protection Agency would not appeal to the buying public was obvious long before the crisis came, yet nobody was ready to do anything about it. Assuming that the clean air goals were too important to be delayed (a rather larger assumption than I am prepared to make, but not an unreasonable one), aggressive government intervention in the marketplace was the only way to avoid frightening unemployment in the automobile industry, with all the ripple effects we have experienced. The need was to move Americans out of inefficient and polluting big cars into small cars that could be more efficient even with the loss of energy to pollution-control devices. A sure-fire stimulus would be the imposition of substantial use taxes on already existing large cars, with the proceeds to be applied to subsidies on the purchase of new small cars suitably less polluting. (A \$100-a-year tax on older large cars would yield in the early years a subsidy of more than \$1,500 each to defray the cost of new small cars.) A great deal of calculating and "planning" would be necessary before so drastic a law could be presented to Congress; none of it was done. Instead, we got all the chatter about the rail transit lines that will not be built.

Our rigidities have been most damaging in manpower planning, where our educational institutions failed to recognize so mountainous a feature of their environment as the giant swing in demography. In 1968, at a Columbia University seminar, I asked Clark Kerr, then beginning his Carnegie studies of higher education, what his committee planned to do about the obvious mismatch of educational effort and manpower needs in the United States. He said they would do nothing—he regarded manpower projections as so inaccurate they could not be accepted as educational guidelines, and as an undue interference with the rights of liberal arts institutions, anyway.

So the universities encouraged young people by the hundreds of thousands to prepare themselves for careers in teaching that would never be available to them. In the meantime, because neither the math department nor the engineering department wanted the trouble, the universities for years left training for computer programming and design in the hands of proprietary schools, even though it was clear as day that society would need millions of men and women with computer expertise before the end of the century. It is not an exclusively American problem. "If demands grow for better health, improved agricultural production, and greater output in technological products," Joseph LaPalombara of Yale writes in a symposium on modernization, "then universities either at home or abroad must produce fewer lawyers and philologists and more doctors, agronomists, agricultural economists, scientists and engineers. Such observations seem self-evident, but . . . the relationship is rarely plain enough to give rise to purposive public policy."

On a more profound level, our increasing use of educational mechanisms as selection devices for the future employment of adults has greatly complicated our efforts to spread opportunities for higher-level employment. Historically, the "educational ladder" had always been more accessible to individuals from certain ethnic or religious backgrounds. Jews, Orientals, Anglo-Saxons, Germans, and Austro-Hungarians had always done better on it as groups than Irish, Italians, Poles, and Spanish. (Though with the decline in ethnic differences in recent years educational differences have diminished, too.) With the arrival of Negro claimants on the scene, however, the cultural selectivity of the educational ladder became crucial to our self-image as a society.

It is now quite clear that the Negro community is not in the lifetimes of men now living going to achieve educational levels anything like as high as those of the white community. The average is a full standard deviation low—that is, the average Negro teen-ager can perform in the normal academic disciplines roughly at the level of the white student who stands around the seventeenth percentile. Only about one-sixth of the

Negro students can be expected to perform as well as the average white. And the figures do not get better. In the early 1960s, I argued in Washington, as a member of the President's Panel on Educational Research and Development, that the effort to integrate schools and improve the chances of Negro students would be justified in the next generation—every educational effort must be judged by its impact on the children of those for whom the effort is made. But the children of those who were in high school in 1963 are now in school themselves, and on the average they are if anything doing even worse.

"Those of us who can still be optimistic about the current status of our intervention in the education of the poor," writes Edmund Gordon of Teachers College, who has given his professional life to the education of the black poor, "can argue that the relatively modest pay-off is less a reflection of inadequate or inappropriate interventions, and more an indication of our inability to adequately measure the positive impact that must be there." That's like saying that if only we had a different gauge for measuring the rainfall we could make the desert bloom: it is a statement of absolute despair.

Because the educational failure of so many Negro students is so apparent, the continued blind insistence on making the schools the focus of the national integration effort is an indefensible abuse of authority by the courts. But it is by no means proved that incapacity at educational skills beyond a certain cut-off point disqualifies from significant accomplishment. There is no backsliding here: incompetency remains the great menace to modern society. Still, the question must be asked: "Incompetency for *what?*" I know personally a number of PhDs whose incompetence is simply beyond question.

Some years ago in *The New Republic* I argued for a law that would require large organizations to reserve at least 10 percent of the places in executive training programs for people who never went to college. This got giggled at, but it really is a good idea. If we are to make a plural society work, we must be prepared to cultivate and measure qualities of energy, judgment, and character that are worth much more in the world of real output than they are in schools. Nor can we seriously hope to twist the schools to serve other than cognitive and normative purposes: every time we try, we produce a contemptible fakery, contemptible because the people who profess it are not perceptive enough to know they are fakes.

It is easy enough to get lip service to the proposition that people can be judged in the job market by what they can do rather than by what they can prove they learned in school, but our increasingly institutionalized, bureaucratized, risk-avoiding society relies more every year on the educational system to slot people for the future. The common cant that increased schooling for more people increases their economic productivity melts under the heat of comparative observation. The two countries with the best continuing economic growth rates (Germany and Japan) have the lowest proportion of their young people in college of all the developed nations; and two of the sickest underdeveloped economies (India and Egypt) draw on the most extensive and prolonged education systems in the Third World. (Until recently, Egypt was actually ahead of Germany in the proportion of young people who completed a full academic secondary program.) Our present and still increasing reliance on educational structures for manpower decisions creates rigidities of social class and *Weltanschauung* that are increasingly harmful both economically and socially.

There are not many agencies in American government that look capable of softening such rigidities without endangering the stability government must nurture. The best candidates would seem to be regulatory agencies, federal or state. They are required to achieve expertise about what really happens in the world under their purview and they are allowed more play in the joints, more exercise of discretion, than any other arm of government. They could, for example, intelligently declare that certain categories of jobs do and others do not require a college education. To some minor extent, this task is already attempted: the FAA decision that pilots did but air traffic controllers did not need a college degree has greatly influenced the allocation of personnel coming into commercial aviation. But it takes policing: in 1975, the FAA backslid, and despite the evidence that college-trained controllers did no better than high-school grads, began to require a college diploma "or equivalent" for jobs in the tower.

The solution—if, indeed, there is a solution—must begin with an assertion that both private and public organizations have an obligation to develop the potential abilities of the people who come to work for them. We are going to have bigger organizations in this country, like it or not (and I don't like it at all); one of the advantages that can be gained from gigantism of enterprise and government is the capacity of the larger organization to train and advance its own people. The Japanese can offer some models for study, and conceivably for adaptation; and our own industrial history argues that American business can restore its own capacity for promotion from within. This is one of the areas where the trade unions will help rather than hinder: one of the first reforms all unions fight for is the "posting" of available jobs that would mean promotion for workers on the shop floor.

But the thing must be for real: the equal opportunity rules up to and including affirmative action are going to prove a dead end as matters are now organized. Too much of the selection process happens in schools, which do not handle this problem well because educators know so little about the real demands of real jobs in what the schools so prissily call "the world of work." The assumption here is that greater numbers of Negroes will be able to compete successfully on the job, in a context of training programs geared to the work to be done. Private corporations are going to have to be paid—and public agencies are going to have to be budgeted—to undertake this sort of functional mobility training with the seriousness the work demands. Without that work, today's stream of court orders and federal guidelines will produce, once their novelty wears off, nothing but cynical boondoggles, social dissonance, and blighted hopes.

5

The first end of government is respect for the trend lines. Even the revolution is never fully acceptable until it becomes, as in Mexico, a permanent revolution. Animal life—including man's —endures because the organism first achieves homeostasis. Flexibility and discretion must be the operating modes, but social stability cannot be achieved through deliberate decision alone, because decision is a process that takes time.

Actions and reactions mediated by collective decision are progressive and change-inducing, necessarily out of phase with the stimuli that produce them. They can succeed only to the extent that they are overlaid upon an established system of semi-automatic reaction that maintains developmental stability. Provided the autonomous system continues to function properly, societies like individuals can adjust cheerfully and take advantage of major alterations of their environment. But significant disturbances in the stabilizers are extremely difficult to remedy without pain and sickness.

This was the villainy of the so-called "full-employment budget" developed by the economists of the Kennedy Administration but carried to destructive extremes only in the Nixon Administration (and, incidentally, in the equally conservative Heath-and-Barber cabinets in Britain in 1970–72). A good part of the secret of the virtually uninterrupted prosperity of 1950–70 had been the automatic swings in the federal budget, which fell into deficit quickly when the economy slowed down, and climbed to near equilibrium (indeed, into surplus, counting what was then an excess of social security tax receipts over social insurance payments) as the economy neared boom conditions.

When the Kennedy-era economists decided they could "fine-tune" the economy, they moved from a situation where the budget would stabilize the economy to a situation where it was assumed that the economy was inherently stable, and would be kept so by agencies other than government. The budget was written not on a projection of expected receipts, but on a projection of what receipts would be if all factors of production were employed at maximum productivity. This left no room for changes in the environment. If electronic calculators displaced mechanical adding machines, to take a trivial example, the government would assume that the excess capacity and unemployment in the mechanical adding machine business was an aberration of the society, which would be remedied more quickly if the deficit in the government budget were greater. But no economy or individual can be kept running at capacity: all change involves frictional loss. Moreover, a modern society with large unmodernized components will have structural difficulties tracing to the very low productivity of some of its people and tools. By insisting that the government prepare its budget as though the economy was always at perfect efficiency in boom conditions, that all the factors of production would be fully employable if the government made the aggregates big enough, the economists guaranteed the spread and growth of inflation. And inflation, as noted in Chapter 4, destroyed the stabilizer.

These pages are being written in London, where competent opinion holds that the institution of credit money is no longer recoverable, that hyperinflation—and, with it, the destruction of both the economic and social foundations of modern democracy—has become inevitable, first in Britain and then throughout the West. I doubt it myself, because a significant psychological stabilizer is still at work, even in London: confronted with the rapid loss of value of their money, people do not hasten to spend it, which the economically rational man would do; instead, they increase the proportion of their income that they save (even at some sacrifice) in the attempt to maintain the purchasing power of their existing savings. Continued drains of real wealth to the Arabs, or continued cowardice by governments that fear unemployment (a manageable problem) more than inflation (an unmanageable one), may still frustrate the operation of this human effort for monetary and societal stability; but so long as savings persist, there is still a chance.

Because economic developments are easily quantified, balance wheel factors and their frustration are more easily observed in the economic statistics—but they can be found everywhere in a modern community. In urbanized developed countries (but not in the Third World), improvements in public health have been matched over the last century by declines in the birthrate; here World War II was the destabilizer. An expansion of educational opportunity matches, at least for a while, the need to keep the young off the job market (and also, incidentally, reduces the birthrate by delaying marriage). The decay of the railroad-based and waterway-served cities produces a decline in value of the underlying land at the urban core, making possible (with government help) urban renewal projects and the construction of road systems to maintain the city's transportation centrality.

Here the stability system was aborted by the politics of symbols rather than realities that disfigured the 1960s; like the ideologues of the Third World who create famine by holding down the price of food for the short-term benefit of the urban proletariat that will later starve, the "community" spokesmen of the 1960s mobilized against all attempts to restructure a city growing increasingly functionless through changes in automotive and communications technology. Even in 1975, when New York City was lurching toward bankruptcy and disintegration, losing jobs and population at an accelerating rate, Representative Bella Abzug announced that she would oppose a private builder's construction of a 20,000-unit housing project on abandoned railroad trackage beside the Hudson River if the apartments were designed for middle-income people (who might help pay the city's bills) and could support it only if the apartments were to be used by charity cases who would further drain the city's vitality.

Natural stabilizers, like competition in the market, can be cruel to the weak—but the consequences of instability are even crueler. Planning government programs "to shake up the Establishment," which was routine operating procedure in the 1960s, will merely increase the opportunity for the strong and unscrupulous to take advantage of instability. Even more disastrously, it produces the kind of leader Harold Laski described as "the remorseless one-idea'd man, who governs us by hewing his way to his goal. He has no time for the open mind. He takes clemency for weakness and difference of opinion for crime. He has a horror of a various civilization and he means by freedom only a stronger kind of chain." We have seen this kind of political leadership at work, left and right, in the America of the last quarter-century.

Natural forces of change in technology and productivity will create motion enough. The task of government is to smooth that motion, and to perform its smoothing functions automatically—like a market, except that government unlike an honest market has purposes, seeks to direct the effects of natural motion, to keep a hand on the scales.

6

The approach to the problems of government that has been outlined in the preceding pages stands subject to two powerful objections. I cannot really answer either, because both are outside the frame of reference in which I work; but I owe them a devoir.

The first is that I leave no way for government to achieve the impossible. I am not, I hope, being frivolous about this. History —everyone's life—presents examples of the impossible come true, and it is only Saint Augustine's impossibility (modernly transmuted to Tertullian's absurdity) that can create a fighting faith. But there is no room for that in the context of surprise reduction.

Neither goodwill nor political action can deliver in a time of declining birthrates the old-age pensions promised at a time of rising birthrates: as the Marxists used to say, the objective situation has changed. In the era of cars and trucks and still-improving telecommunications, the recent city built on the convergence of rail lines or waterways cannot be reconstructed, any more than one can resurrect the ancient walled city built on safety and the liberty of the physically defensible marketplace. Even after the most enlightened and successful urban renewal, art and commerce and sporting events and even government will continue to spread themselves around the satellites, leaving the city less than it used to be—though not so little as it may be if we fail to do what can be done.

As the new land to be opened up and new resources to be uncovered diminish in proportion to what is already in use, the support of a rising standard of living or rising population requires great improvements in efficiency and great reductions in waste. Greater efficiency means further division of labor and hierarchical organization to envision and control the abstractions that express large-scale productive effort; reduced waste means government intervention in the price/cost system to stimulate the recycling that seems more expensive today. The libertarians of both left and right are calling their wares from the dust heap of history.

The passage of time forecloses options, in the life of societies as well as of individuals. The white man's God may or may not be dead, but the Great Spirit of the American Indian is permanently departed to his Happy Hunting Ground, and the grim logic of "modernize or die" applies to the tropical nations today even more rigorously than it did in the 1950s, when everyone was mouthing it. Technology and social organization are not a smorgasbord from which one chooses only what one likes or can easily digest. Reduced infant mortality, increased longevity, the introduction of manufactured goods, easy transportation, telecommunications—you can't, you really can't go home again. Much is cyclical in human history; but technological advance and material expectation are reversible only by catastrophe.

The other objection I cannot answer is that the principles I propose will not fundamentally redistribute the benefits and rewards generated within a society. There is no blinking the fact that the patterns of stimulus and obstacle envisioned in these pages seek to engage the self-interest of the more competent fraction of the community, not "to promote their own destruction" (they are in the end too clever for that, and those who seek their destruction are too foolish), but to advance the interests of the society at large, others as well as, perhaps not so much as, themselves.

It is no great trick in any society to change the identity of the individuals who get the largest share of the goodies. Revolutions do this quickly, but in most western societies normal process moves wealth and position to new hands just as effectively. Some great twentieth-century English families trace back to Elizabethan roots, but few of the great country houses now in the hands of Britain's National Trust had been owned as long as a century by the family that finally deeded them to public use. In America, the 1920s saw proof of the already clichéd line about "shirtsleeves to shirtsleeves in three generations"; and in the hippie movement of the 1960s we saw the variant of pushcarts to pushcarts in an equivalent period of time.

But while the personnel of the top crowd changes fairly rapidly, the income share that goes to the top is likely to change only slowly, and will usually reflect changes in technology and social organization more than political action. In societies where defense is taken as the first need, a military aristocracy grabs what seems to later generations a shocking share—feudal Europe and Japan, more recently Moghul India, Imperial Turkey, the Latin American "republics." In societies where productive enterprise is highly interdependent, where the business of the country is business (or, what amounts to the same thing, the construction of socialism), significant contributions are made by increasingly large fractions of the community and improvements in efficiency generate larger absolute income for all (more quickly in capitalist societies, with their systemic capacity for the correction of error, than in oligarchical or socialist societies). But the directors and the proprietors of the more important magics—the people whose performance most affects the income or happiness or safety of everybody else—continue to gain what many consider disproportionate rewards. I see little reason to believe that these ratios are much disturbed by mere political change. The British Labor Party is trying hard, and the middle classes feel themselves ground down, but it will obviously come to very little. After the revolution is over and things settle down it turns out that the new fellows in the Kremlin enjoy perks not unlike those of their predecessors, and the means of delivering the rewards have changed more than the rewards themselves.*

Obviously, there are in all societies scoundrels and groups of scoundrels—and fortunately placed individuals—who grab off more than they can be said to contribute. Moreover, patterns of distribution tend to have a persistence even in the face of technological or institutional change that removes their reason for being. So long as the money system is operated as a control —that is, in the absence of inflation, which hides the need to make real choices—there is every reason for all who feel themselves insufficiently rewarded to push for what Samuel Gompers compendiously described as "more." To say that the distribution arrangements are consonant with the economic contribution of the factors, after all, is merely to say that the pricing system is working properly. Adjustments that bring re-

---

*An unusually explicit example of disparities under conditions of Communist equality comes to hand in an article about the new Soviet cruise ship *Belorussiya* in the British magazine *Marine and Air Catering:* "Captain and chief engineer both have suites that look out forward. Immediately behind each is a small cabin for a second officer. Aft of that again on the starboard side is accommodation for the 'assistant captain' and for the first officer. On the port side there is a cabin for the chief cook and the purser's suite with day-room, bedroom, and office. Other navigating and engineering officers and chief radio officer are amidships, with a sports hall aft. . . . One has to plummet down to the fourth and fifth decks before finding the tiny cabins that accommodate the crew. . . . Part of the crew is housed alongside the main car deck, together with laundry facilities, overall stores, garbage room, etc. The rest are one deck below. The cabins will hold two or four, although it is sincerely hoped that this will not be the case, as some of them have an area little larger than the captain's bathroom. . . ."

wards into line with contributions can provoke great bursts of economic activity, as demonstrated in France after 1968. Adjustments that take the reward structure too far out of line with contributions produce economic decay, as can be seen in Uruguay in the 1950s and in New York City in the 1970s.

Political decisions usually determine only whether a reality is expressed in one set of abstractions or another set of abstractions. The result may indeed be nontrivial: money itself is an abstraction, and the social harm that can be done if the money system fails is roughly comparable to the social harm that can be done by civil war. Even without its propensity to disaster, politics may be more effective than I think it is in converting its acknowledged individual who-gets-what function into a statistical distribution of rewards among functional groups. But the worldwide modern contempt for politics and politicians expresses, I think, general realization that the daily life of man is not vastly affected—certainly not vastly improved—by the operation of this largely parasitic generation of "power."

The reader may have noted that this portmanteau word "power" has rarely appeared in these pages. I use it with the greatest reluctance: I do not know what it means, and I do not believe anybody else knows, either. In nineteenth-century legal opinion it was the operative for "function" (i.e., "police power, war powers"), but that restrictive sense was lost and now the word is what the Africans call a juju, a convenient magical way to explain events that otherwise don't make sense. What we mean now when we use the word "power" is usually authority —that is, some person or organization has been authorized through some known process to make arrests or assess taxes or fire the office boy or write the editorial. Though authority can be abused, we normally say it is "exercised." When we speak of power, the common accompanying verb will be "abuse." I think that what we really mean when we say "power" is the arbitrary use of authority *ultra vires*—beyond the authorizing rules. Thus the OPEC countries have the power to set international oil prices, the policemen's union has the power to make the city unlivable, the teacher has the power to suspend a pupil who gets on her nerves. In those terms, of course, Acton's aphorism has to be correct. Authority comes by right; power comes by wrong.

My position, anyway, is that what government does in the United States these days is too important to be controlled by politics as customarily defined. There are a number of things that really must get done, mostly by government or under government urging, in the next half-dozen years, and I could not care less whether the government that does them calls itself conservative or liberal or radical, Democratic, Republican, American, Socialist Worker, or Libertarian. If we can get the substance right, I can put up with almost any style.

7

Finally, we really must look ahead; even a peer into the murk is better than just stumbling along. It takes courage for the individual, because everyone's life comes out badly—but institutions can hope to survive, and they have calls upon us. In its educational role (and a large part of what government does is really educational), government must seek to lift the time horizons of the nonexpert public, and emphasize the future consequences of current decisions.

Simply to write the words is to feel a hopeless fool, for all the trend lines go the other way. Anytime anybody pauses to consider, the advertising that fills our lives nips anxiously at his heels. Living for today has been the path of least resistance at least since we have written records of human attitudes; and one of the things modern society has bought with its affluence is the easy acceptance (indeed, the active promotion) of "doing your own thing." In a democratic society the pressure on government to keep things as they are but make them better—which means the constantly increasing expenditure of current resources on current consumption—becomes almost irresistible.

Distribution rather than production becomes the focus of concern. Inflation is merely one of the symptoms of societal disease; among the others are commercial, political, and sexual dishonesty.

It is obviously impossible to deliver to the living the benefits of investment in the future; and I fear it is impossible to allocate the costs "equitably." If a sewage-treatment plant must be built (and it must) the people who live on and near the site chosen for the plant pay the costs much more than those in other neighborhoods who merely pay the taxes. Charles Kindleberger noted that the British economists of the nineteenth century promoted free trade as a benefit for the entire world, while Bismarck "cynically regarded free trade as the weapon of a country with a technological lead. One can envy," Kindleberger continues, "the special interest which is able to clothe its arguments in general terms—just as the last refuge of a scoundrel is patriotism—while other special groups whose interests cannot be identified with the commonweal are obliged either to cling to patently thin general arguments or reveal themselves as selfish." Kindleberger underestimated both the capacity for self-deception in politically advanced communities and the suggestibility of the press. Thus the residents of the West Side of Manhattan can oppose the construction of a convention center and the repair of the highway along the river— both desperately needed for the future economy of New York City—while wrapping themselves in an impenetrable mantle of progressivism and social concern. Micawber not Marx has become the prophet of the modern American Left.

It is easy to make fun, but in fact we deal with painful choices that cut much deeper than our usual terms of discussion. People pay attention to the future for three reasons. One is greed for future possessions or pleasures; but today we have buy now–pay later, and consumer credit (quite apart from mortgage credit) that adds up to more than two months' total personal income for the country as a whole. A second reason is a felt need to put something aside for survival in times of trouble, for unemployment, illness, old age, and (a most important factor in poor and primitive societies) burial. I yield to no one in my affection for social security, unemployment insurance, and (within limits) health insurance; but we must face the fact that the development of the welfare state permits people to slough their concerns about the prospect onto the strong if sloping shoulders of government (which in turn relies on future generations to pay the bills). People who get used to this attitude lose their willingness to think about the future, to accept burdens today for their own (or the general) good tomorrow.

The third and best reason to care about the future is the decent parent's desires and hopes for his children. We have been told now by fifty years of psychiatrists what an awful thing it is when parents seek to live vicariously through their children; we have forgotten what an awful thing it is when they do not. We regard "love" as an instant phenomenon, not as a word that acquires meaning only within a frame of time. We make an aimlessness, and call it alienation. We ought to be ashamed of ourselves.

Man's commitment to the future is through his seed; his purpose is the passing on of the genetic inheritance that is his alone. He should care what happens to it; he should not wish it to have no more than equal opportunity with all other seed; and in fact he doesn't. Hence the hypocrisy that accompanies all pious assurance of a commitment to equal opportunity; the politicians who support busing and send their own children to private school; the rapid abandonment by families who can flee of neighborhoods that no longer seem "safe for the children." When the state tells parents that they must send their children away from their home neighborhoods to schools that are in fact unsafe schools—and this is precisely what the state has been doing in thousands of communities for the last decade—the state tells parents that they must be willing to sacrifice the future that does and should matter most to them for the sake of a current abstraction that is fashionable among judges. It tells them not to think about the future, not to provide for their children, to live selfishly in the present. One should not then be surprised if they do so—and if, forbidden to act on their need to protect their children, they lose charity.

I am not, I hope, underestimating the dimensions of the problem the courts have sought to solve. I was for five years chairman of a local school board for a district that was two-thirds Negro and Puerto Rican, and I know in my gut as well as in my head that the tragedy of being black in America is one's inability to protect one's children—that the short time horizons that afflict the Negro community are largely the result of their entrapment in an environment that destroys their children's lives. There is no national need greater than the assurance—achievable in part by residential desegregation—that Negroes who contribute productively to the society can pass on to their children the normal rewards of their success.

Our school board initiated and fought through a busing program that brought East Harlem children to, among others, the schools where my boys went. To extend to parents the opportunity for their children to go to a school they consider better than the one previously available is to my mind an entirely positive function of government. To force parents to send children to a school they consider less good than the one previously available is a decision fraught with major negative consequences. We are, I fear, going to pay a terrible price for having placed on our young people the entire burden of socializing the rural Negro come to the city. But the worst of it has been the rebuke to the best instincts of the family, and to the desire to look to the future, which is always closely linked to the children.

The futurology that bemused so many people just a few years ago was made trivial by the lack of perceived linkages between what happened yesterday, what is happening today, and what was assumed to be our destiny in the year 2000. The notion that today's decisions restrict tomorrow was scarcely there at all. Instead, the Lord—science, technology, changes in attitudes that were presumed to be coming because the newspapers said so—would somehow provide. The environmentalist movement especially was trivialized by the failure to think seriously of the multitude of interrelated changes that make a future, by the demand for unidimensional environmental impact statements that ask in the end, if you read them, how a single given change will affect a straight-line projection of the present.

It was profoundly discouraging in early 1975 to watch political, business, and labor leaders wrestle with the consequences of the economic decline. So far as could be seen from the outside—from the face they presented to the public—our leaders had nothing on their minds but the reconstitution of the immediate past. But we were in trouble because of the imbalances in the economy and the society that characterized that recent past; the recession was a sewage system for carrying away the consequences of those mistakes. Government's task was to protect the innocent, the employees of those who had made the mistakes, without impeding the flushing out of the guilty—the speculators, the corporations, the banks, the featherbedding unions, and, yes, the overstretched municipalities, all of which had "planned" a future that did not arrive. Instead, the struggle was entirely to pump the balloon back to its old shape, and let the next Congress—the next president of the company, chairman of the bank, president of the union, mayor of the city—deal with the worse deformations or even the bust that would inevitably result.

7

Assuming the human animal that is and the state of our technology, I have no vision of the Just Society greatly different from what I might expect if we ran what we have more honestly, more charitably, and more intelligently than we do today. But we really must be more honest, more charitable, and especially more intelligent. I know I have given away a great deal by accepting what seems to me the truth that greed and familial loyalties are *and should be* the usual motive forces in human society; I give it away gladly, saving only charity, which is still the greatest of the achieved virtues, and the pleasures of self-esteem through craft, which is a subcategory of greed. I have experienced the wild joy of leading a "mass movement" of protest, and I hope never to yield to such delectable temptations again. Unselfish dedication to a cause ought not to be idealized, for there is no limit to the evil such dedication can do. Forty years ago, Geoffrey Crowther wrote from England on "the passionate devotion with which a whole people will embrace an opportunity to give service to their community"; the people he was writing about were the Germans, and the devotion was Nazism. You can ask more from people than their natural abilities will supply, and you may get it; if you ask more than natural motivation will supply, you loose demons.

Christopher Jencks and his colleagues, with admirable and engaging scholarly honesty, have revealed how remarkably open and mobile American society has been; at the end of their book *Inequality* they can attribute most of the inequalities that exist only to chance. The argument is not wholly persuasive (genetic endowments of energy are not "chance"), but it does effectively destroy the case for dramatic fundamental change. We are not going to eliminate chance—or mongolism, or senility, or inequalities in strength, intelligence, judgment, reaction time, sexual attractiveness, speed afoot, social status, income. A world of clones from even the most amusing people would not be very interesting to live in, anyway.

Despite the billboarded announcements of the sociologists, the pace of change has not been speeding up. Indeed, if change is seen as deviation from the trend line, it has slowed down considerably. What happened in the world in their lifetimes was more surprising, I think, to the generation born in 1880 than it was to the generation born in 1910; and for those born in 1940 the real changes during the twenty years since they began to pay serious attention to the world around them have been, if you think about it, surprisingly small. We are still living on the intellectual capital of the early years of this century:

major change has come upon us since World War II only in biology, geology, astronomy, communications technology, artificial intelligence, and race relations. It is not an ignoble record, but it is by no means the revolution observed by the age cohort of 1880, who lived through the introduction of universal electrification, flying, the automobile, radio, plastics, antibiotics, divorce, the departure of the kings, Einstein, Freud and Lenin, Schoenberg, Joyce and Picasso, the welfare state, and changes in the substratum of science and social science that are still "modern" forty, fifty, and sixty years after their proclamation.

I do not quarrel with the proposition that we live in a time of the winding down of the modern impulse, but there is still a lot of strength in the mainspring. Barring wars, hyperinflation or climatic change, what happens next in the cataclysmic sense is still a long way off in the modernized countries. But what will happen next as the persistent forces of our culture exert their continuing pressure is right around the corner. Bismarck once observed the God looks after idiots, drunks, and the United States of America, but that was a long time ago. I think we are on our own, now, and the time has come to cultivate the reality principle.

"Seek simplicity," Whitehead insisted, "and distrust it." The world is truly complicated, but there is something to be said for being human and alive, conditions that still offer certain possibilities and still impose certain obligations, the first of which is to think ahead. Nobody, as the politicians say, is making any promises; I do believe that with a little luck we can channel predictable change; improve as a society our ability to recognize, admit, and correct mistakes; and come to tolerant terms as individuals with the well-known but ever-humiliating facts of our humanity, and our personal mortality, and the immanence of our posterity.

Explanation
and Acknowledgment

I began work on this book in Geneva, where I was more or less stranded in a hotel room for the better part of a week, because both the people I was to see on business and the friends I was to visit had gone to the mountains for the Wednesday-to-Tuesday period that modern Europe consecrates to the consideration of the crucifixion and resurrection of Christ. Some had gone to the seashore, to Italy.

This was Easter 1973, and I was in a fairly foul mood about both American society and its critics. I was working on a book about banks and bankers, and could see big economic trouble ahead; I had been serving on a commission to explore reforms in secondary education, and was heartsick about the decline in the overall quality of our high schools that was and still is visible to anyone who cares to look; because my most recently published book had been about television, I was still paying attention to what appears on the little screen, always a source of dyspepsia; and I had just lived through the 1972 elections. Both the steaks and the Beaujolais at the Café de Paris cost about three times as much (in dollars) as they had on my previous stay in this city. *The New York Times Magazine* reached me by cable, to commission an article about educational testing, in which I would of course be sure to cover what the editors considered the three most important points, all three of them meaningless or factually wrong or both. I was traveling alone. It snowed, moistly.

So I sat down and wrote about fifty highly irritated pages, the gravamen of which was that the 1960s had really ended, about three years before; and that the collection of 1960s attitudes that still dominated American art and politics and higher education, nonfunctional even in their own time, had now become in every sense a drag. The Age of Rubbish, Dick Hofstadter had called it; but it was an age of gilded rubbish, which confused people, made them think there was a Gilded Age. Man can live with a tragic vision (by God, he'd better, as Carlyle suggested); but not with inconsequence. On my return to New York, I showed these fifty pages to Ann Harris, my editor, who thought there was a book in them. I churned on grumblingly for another hundred pages, and was about to complete what would have been a very bad book when the Arabs in one week knocked us out of the 1960s. Mrs. Harris and I agreed, I suspect with relief on both sides, that the project should lay over for a while, and that we should look at it again in a year or so and see what had survived.

Surprisingly, a lot of it was still there: some of the salt had lost its savor, but there seemed to be meat underneath. One man's meat, of course; that can't be helped. My job, it seemed to me, was to cut out some of the irritability (which an unkind reader might call snottiness); focus the material constructively on understanding rather than on the demolition of fashionable stupidities; smooth a few transitions; and make sure I was giving credit where credit was due, to the men who had written the books and articles that had moved my thinking to where I had arrived. That last was going to be a pleasure; the one purpose I am sure can be served by a book of this kind is to call to the attention of a wider audience the work of men who seem to me to be giants in our time—economists like Harry Johnson, William Baumol and Charles Kindleberger, a sociologist-geographer like Marion Levy, historians like Lynn White and Herbert Heaton, law professors like Harry Kalven and Milton Katz, engineers like Harvey Brooks and Robert Fano, government affairs analysts like Aaron Wildavsky and James Webb.

Mrs. Harris was after something more. The racing writer Joe Palmer once told a story about the handicapper of a western track who put top weight on what he considered the best of the older horses on the grounds, and persisted in assigning that weight through week after week when the horse failed to win and the owner bitterly complained. Came the last day of the meeting and the richest stakes, and the horse, under top weight, won by ten panels of fence; the handicapper, Palmer noted, had "made him try." That was Mrs. Harris's mission: week after week, through revision after revision, by means of firm (never unfriendly, but firm) memos about this word, that sentence, the other paragraph—and, indeed, this thought, that explanation, the other suggestion—she worked to make me try. It was a virtuoso performance in an oft-practiced but rarely mastered art. Whether we have a winner now, I don't know; as Count Danilo observed when the Merry Widow told him he danced divinely, *Man tut was man kann.* But there can be no doubt that both the speed and the cohesion of the preceding pages have been vastly enhanced. I certainly wouldn't—almost certainly couldn't—have done it by myself. Thank you, Ann.

About the Author

Martin Prager Mayer was born in New York in 1928, and was graduated from Harvard, where he majored in economics and also studied philosophy and music.

After working as a reporter and editor for several publications, he became a free-lance writer in 1954. He is the author of two novels and six major reportorial studies: *Wall Street: Men and Money; Madison Avenue, U.S.A.; The Schools; The Lawyers; About Television;* and *The Bankers.* His articles on education, business, television, music, law, finance and other subjects have appeared in a wide variety of magazines.

From 1961 to 1965 Mr. Mayer was a member of the Panel on Educational Research and Development in the Executive Office of the President, and from 1962 to 1967 he was the chairman of a New York City local school board. His work has been supported at various times by the American Council of Learned Societies, the Twentieth Century Fund, the Sloan Foundation, and the William Nelson Cromwell Foundation.

Mr. Mayer is married to the writer and scholar Ellen Moers. They and their two sons live in New York.